UNIVERSITY SCHOOL LIBRARY
UNIVERSITY OF WYOMING

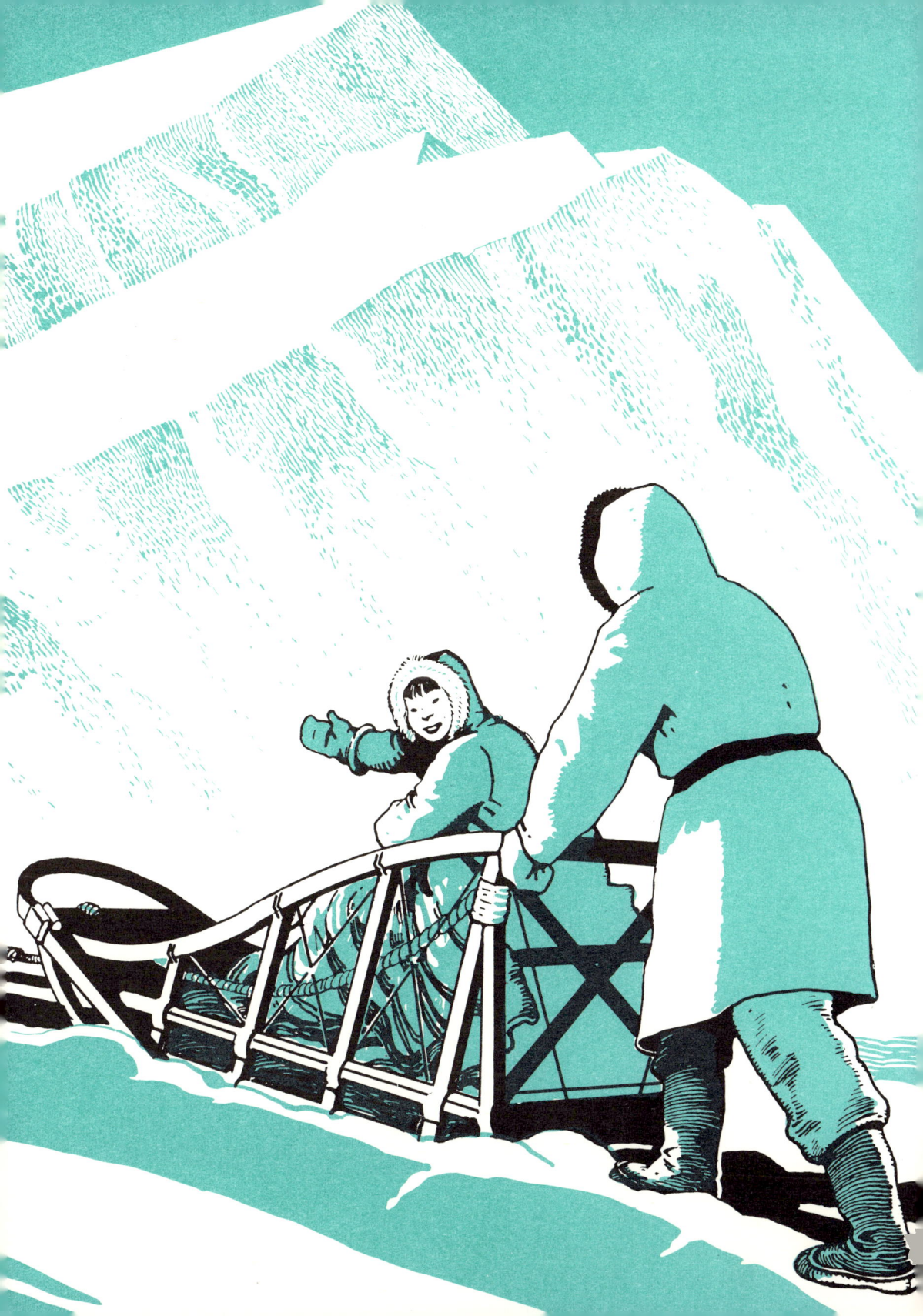

All About the Arctic and Antarctic

The Arctic and the Antarctic—the extreme northern and southern regions of the earth—have always fascinated people in other parts of the world.

This book tells about weather, land formations, ocean currents, plants, animals, and human beings in the polar regions, as well as the bold explorations that have made this knowledge possible.

Armstrong Sperry is the author of a number of books for young people, including the Newbery Medal winner *Call It Courage*.

All About
THE ARCTIC AND ANTARCTIC

Written and Illustrated by Armstrong Sperry

Random House / New York

© COPYRIGHT, 1957, BY ARMSTRONG SPERRY

All rights reserved under International and Pan-American Copyright Conventions. Published in New York by Random House, Inc., and simultaneously in Toronto, Canada, by Random House of Canada, Limited.

MANUFACTURED IN THE UNITED STATES OF AMERICA

This title was originally catalogued by the Library of Congress as follows:

Sperry, Armstrong, 1897–
    All about the Arctic and Antarctic, written and illustrated by Armstrong Sperry. New York, Random House [1957]
    146 p. illus. 24 cm. (Allabout books, A-20)

1. Arctic regions.   2. Antarctic regions.   ɪ. Title.

PZ9.S783Al   57—7518
Library of Congress   [67b²3]

Trade Ed.: ISBN: 0-394-80220-9   Lib. Ed.: ISBN: 0-394-90220-3

Contents

1. On Top of the World   3
2. Weather, Wind, Ice and Permafrost   13
3. Arctic Spring and Summer   23
4. The Long Winter Night   35
5. The Treasure Chest of the Arctic   44
6. Fur-Bearers of the North   57
7. Creatures of the Arctic Sea   71
8. Arctic Birds That Come and Go   84
9. The Eskimo's Greatest Friend   92
10. Towering Peaks and Icy Depths   103
11. Exploring the World of the Antarctic   112
12. Mysterious Sights and Sounds   117
13. Antarctic Wild Life   123
14. Operation Deep-Freeze   134
    Index   141

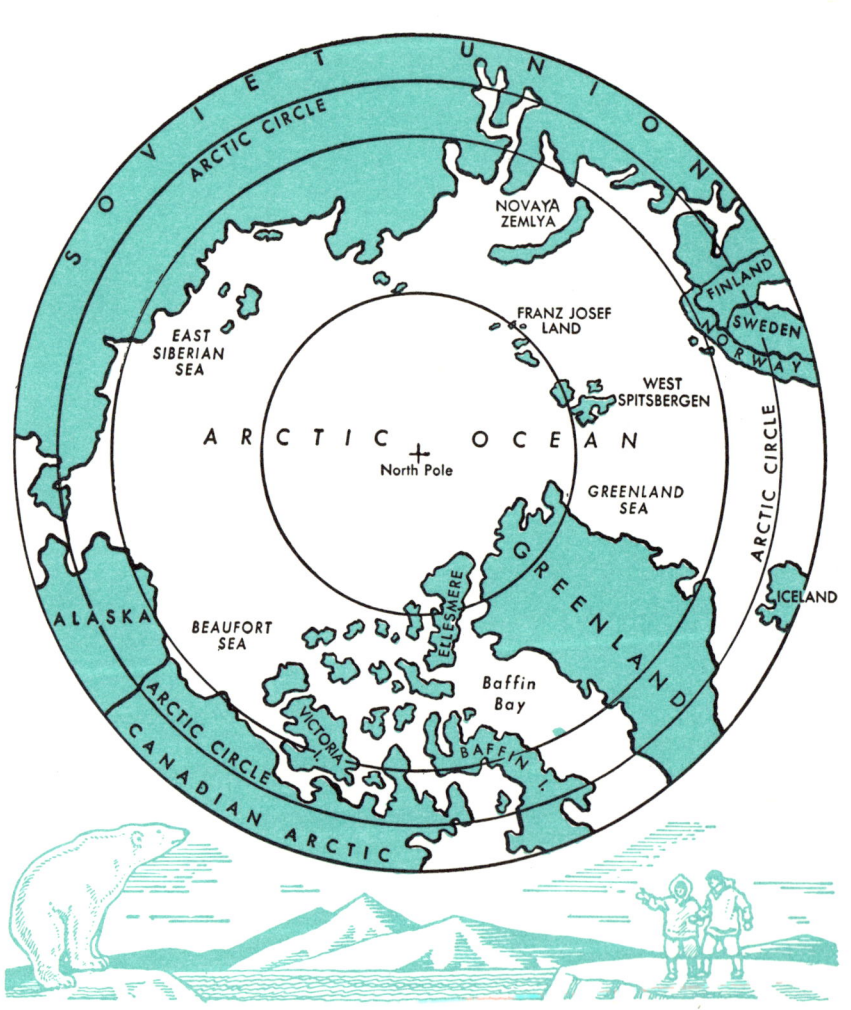

1.
On Top of the World

A bird's-eye view of the top of our world is shown on the map opposite. With the North Pole as its center, the Arctic Circle has a diameter of 3,300 miles. Caught within the edge of this Circle lie slices of Alaska, Canada, Greenland, northern Europe and Siberia. Actually the Arctic Circle is only an imaginary line on the map. North of this map line the midnight sun may be seen for a full twenty-four hours in late June. And in late December the same area has twenty-four hours of darkness with no sunshine at all.

Another way of marking the Arctic region is by what we call the tree line. This doesn't show on a map, but it can be seen by any traveler. Trees can't survive

All About the Arctic and Antarctic

in extreme cold. So there is a northern limit beyond which no trees grow. Here the earth is black, boggy ground. Beneath the surface it is permanently frozen. But great areas are covered with reindeer moss and various grasses. This part of the Arctic is known as the tundra. Here and there tiny dwarfed willows may be found. This is the reason why the Indians call the tundra "the land of little sticks."

When you look at a map of the Arctic, you see that many slices of land lie within the rim of the Circle. Like a pack of Eskimo dogs surrounding a bear, these fringes of land encircle the vast Polar Basin. Here more than 5,000,000 square miles of water cover the roof of the world. In some places the water is 15,000 feet deep.

But the Polar Basin is not a flat, unbroken plain of ice. As new ice forms under the bottom of the old ice, it heaves upward, cracking the surface. The result is a tangle of broken sheets of floating ice, called ice floes. Driven by wind and tide, these floes are forever churning and grinding. Now they freeze together; again they crack apart. They form a jigsaw puzzle of pinnacles, caverns and precipices.

This monstrous ice field is called the Polar Ice Pack. The most surprising thing about it is that it is moving

On Top of the World

constantly throughout the year. Because of the rotation of the earth, the Polar Ice Pack drifts from Alaska and Siberia toward Greenland.

Being almost completely surrounded by land, the Polar Basin is more truly a landlocked sea than an ocean. It is small indeed when compared with the Pacific or the Atlantic. For this reason the words "Arctic Ocean" are now being replaced on many maps by the name "Arctic or Polar Sea." This sea separates North America from Asia, much as the Mediterranean separates Europe from Africa.

Surprisingly enough, the water of the Arctic Sea has different temperatures at different depths. The top layer of water—some 650 feet deep—has temperatures around 30° F. This water has a relatively low salt content, due to rain, melted snow, and vast quantities of river water. Beneath this, a second layer of water—2,500 feet deep—is warmer and saltier. This water is carried by the Gulf Stream from the Atlantic Ocean, up into the Arctic Basin. Below this second layer, there is again cold water, filling the whole Basin to the bottom, with temperatures around 30° F.

The system of currents in the Arctic Sea is one of the most interesting geographical features of the region.

All About the Arctic and Antarctic

For beneath those vast acres of ice, there are streams of warmer or colder water that flow in predictable directions throughout the Arctic Sea.

The map shows that the only large opening into the Polar Basin is the Greenland Sea. This connects the Arctic Sea with the oceans to the south. Through this sea comes a current of warm Atlantic water, which penetrates the Polar Sea. Because of this warm current of water, the Arctic world is mild and gentle as compared to the Antarctic world.

This current and many others, sweeping in various directions, are important in the development of the Arctic. They influence ice conditions as well as the weather of the whole Northland. In addition, they affect the routes of navigation and the lives of the people who live on the land encircling the Polar Basin.

Within the Arctic Circle there is at least one day out of the year when the sun doesn't rise above the horizon. As you approach the North Pole, the number of sunless days increases. Finally, at the Pole itself, there are six months of almost total darkness each year. But for every day when the sun doesn't rise, there is a day six months later when the sun doesn't sink below the horizon.

To people who dwell in warmer regions this seems

On Top of the World

almost unbelievable. What makes this the land of the midnight sun? You will understand the reason if you remember that the earth tilts to one side as it spins around the sun. This means that sometimes the North Pole is leaning toward the sun, sometimes away from it. In June the North Pole leans toward the sun. In the Arctic the sun never sets during that period. It is always above the horizon. There is sunshine even at midnight. But in the winter, the North Pole is tilted away from the sun, and there is darkness day and night.

Sometimes during the long Arctic night, strange

The North Pole leans toward the sun in June.

All About the Arctic and Antarctic

flickering lights may be seen in the sky. There will be a steady glow with beams that shoot upward toward the middle of the heavens. This is the famous aurora borealis or northern lights. Usually the aurora is made up of luminous bands of pale light. Sometimes it is tinged with yellow or red, more rarely with green or violet. But whatever the color, there is always movement. These strange light beams are believed to be caused by electrically charged particles shot away from the sun.

Many people still believe that the entire Arctic is like the Polar Basin. They think of it as a wild and remote region of perpetual ice and snow, where during months of darkness the howl of the wolf competes with that of the wind. The myth of the hostile North has been like a snowball racing downhill, growing larger and larger. Of course, there are areas where conditions are truly harsh. But the Arctic is a land of surprising contrasts. In some regions Eskimos wear fur-lined parkas the year around, and planes land on skis even in midsummer. But in other places—parts of Alaska, for example, and the Canadian Arctic—crops may be grown in abundance during the summer months of continuous daylight. Even in the extreme north of Greenland,

On Top of the World

barely 600 miles from the Pole, nearly two hundred varieties of mosses and plants flourish.

Often we hear about the howling blizzards of the Northland. But a great explorer named Nansen, one of the pioneers in the Arctic, considered the Arctic to be less stormy than any other region of equal size in the world. He gave maximum wind velocity, for three years at sea, as 50 miles per hour. Stefansson, another great Arctic explorer, states that he has never seen a greater than 50-mile wind when more than 50 miles from shore. Yet a hurricane in the United States may travel 100 miles an hour! On the coastal plains of the Northland the air is so dry that less snow falls there than in Richmond, Virginia.

Today this huge area of ice-capped mountains, lakes, boggy plains and pack ice is a link between the continents. The shortest air route between Europe and America lies across the top of the world. From Tokyo to London, from New York to Shanghai, the quickest short cut is via the North Pole. You can prove this yourself with a piece of string on a globe.

A new era in commercial aviation began on November 19, 1952, when a Scandinavian Airlines DC-6 Super-Cloudmaster made the first trial run from Los

The shortest air route to Asia lies across the North Pole.

Angeles to Denmark. It flew via northwest Greenland and covered almost 10,000 miles in little more than twenty-four hours.

But strange things happen as you fly north over the roof of the world. The compass, for example, becomes untrustworthy. As you go farther north, the needle begins to spin aimlessly, sometimes pointing east when it means west. If you have three different compasses in the same plane, each may swing in a different direction. The fact is, when you are above the North Pole itself, there is no north! You have gone as far north as possible. East and west have vanished also. From the North

On Top of the World

Pole, *every direction is south*. Under such conditions, it is no wonder that an ordinary compass doesn't know how to behave!

For Polar flying the compass has been replaced by a gyroscopic instrument called the Polar Path Gyro. This is a direction-holding device rather than a direction-finding one. The navigator sets his instrument and throws a switch. And the gyro does the rest, but not entirely. For even this magical instrument is subject to error. The turning of the earth confuses it. The plane's nose may be leveled directly at Tokyo when the gyro is set; but the earth meanwhile is spinning beneath the plane. Soon the same direction in space no longer points toward Tokyo. So the careful pilot must reset his gyro at frequent intervals, checking it against other instruments. He takes bearings on the sun, measures the wind drift, records barometric pressure. In short he checks everything against everything else.

This confusion of space and direction in the high Arctic has made our old-fashioned maps useless for Polar flight. The new flying maps look like the squared-off blueprints of a modern city—broad, straight highways across the Arctic sky.

Today the Arctic becomes vitally important as two

All About the Arctic and Antarctic

tremendous construction jobs are being completed. One, referred to as White Alice, is a network of microwave links connecting isolated communities and defense installations. The other is known as the DEW Line (the Distant Early Warning Line). This will flash the first warning of unidentified planes approaching from the North. The DEW Line was built by the United States at an estimated cost of $450,000,000. From Alaska to the edge of Greenland, it runs within 400 miles of the North Pole. Radar stations and construction camps now dot a vast area of hitherto uncharted wilderness. Almost overnight the North Polar regions have become the center of our world.

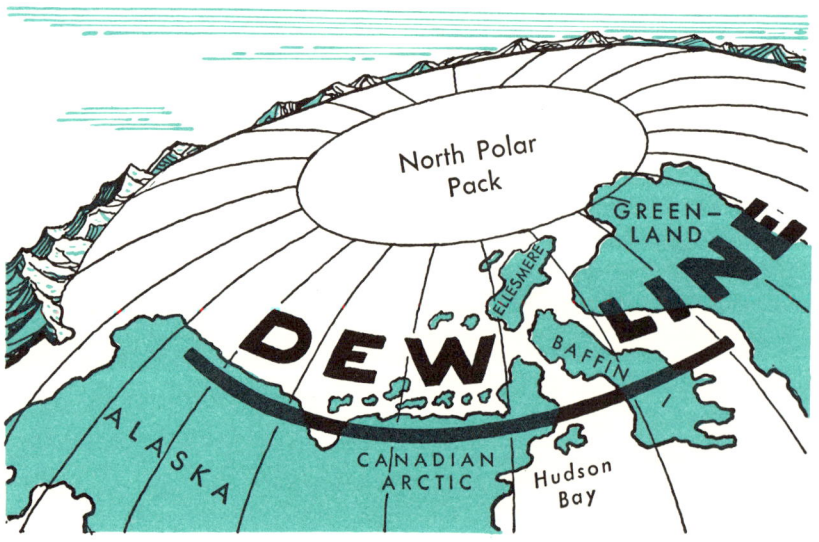

2.

Weather, Wind, Ice and Permafrost

In the Arctic everything depends on the weather. Like the region and its people, the weather shows great variety. Temperatures at the North Pole are warmer on the average than those of Northern Siberia and Central Greenland. In fact the coldest spot known on earth is Oimekon, Siberia, which lies more than 200 miles *south* of the Arctic Circle.

Contrary to popular belief, the Northland has great intensities of both cold and heat. The hottest Arctic weather recorded is at Fort Yukon, Alaska, a few miles

All About the Arctic and Antarctic

north of the Circle. There it was 100° in the shade. That record has been reached only once. But summer temperatures of 95° have been recorded many times in various parts of the Arctic. Summer heat of 85° to 90° may be expected in the far North whenever the following conditions prevail: low land, more than 100 miles distant from the sea, with remote snow-clad mountains. The coldest recorded temperature is 94° below zero—at Verkhoyansk, Siberia, fifty miles north of the Arctic Circle. Like Oimekon, Verkhoyansk is on low land enclosed by mountains, remote from the moderating influences of the sea.

Extreme cold is the greatest barrier to industrial development in the North. At sub-zero temperatures, engines have to be thawed out by blowtorches. Water condenses and freezes in the fuel line of aircraft or bulldozer. Even antifreeze turns to slush. Rubber tires split open. The blade of an ax must be warmed before it is used or it will splinter like glass. A sharply struck nail shivers into fragments. The moisture on a match head freezes. So does the ink in your fountain pen. Camera shutters jam, film cracks.

As the thermometer drops, steam rises from a dog or a caribou, so that the animal can scarcely be seen from a distance of thirty feet—the result of cold air touching

Weather, Wind, Ice and Permafrost

a warm surface. A running reindeer leaves a trail of smokelike steam behind it.

But above all, extreme cold affects the human body. Additional layers of clothing offset to some extent the heat loss; but the results make clumsy, impractical garments. Nothing the white man has designed is so efficient as the Eskimo's caribou parka or shirt, his bear skin trousers and sealskin boots. Because the parka is loose enough for proper ventilation, it permits a circulation of air which prevents sweating. This is very important, for any moisture at low temperature freezes and may cause real suffering. The armholes of a parka are cut large enough for a man to withdraw his arms and warm his hands against his body. The entire outfit weighs around ten pounds and is practically cold-proof. Wolverine fur is used to frame the hood. On any other type of fur, a man's breath will freeze into a mass of icy particles. For this reason, polar explorers seldom grow beards when there is any opportunity to shave. Breath condenses in a beard and freezes into a mask of ice.

In the Arctic the colder the air the easier it is to see for a great distance. Sometimes this confuses an explorer. For what appears to be a small hill two or three miles distant may turn out to be a mountain thirty miles away.

Men face real difficulty because of mirages too. These

are reflections of objects lying below the horizon. Sometimes they magnify and distort such everyday things as sleds and dogs. As a result of the so-called *loom*, Nansen nearly shot one of his favorite dogs. He mistook it for a polar bear.

The *loom* depends on rapid changes of density of the air with increasing altitude. When a dense cold layer gives way to a warmer layer at a lower density, the light rays are bent back toward the earth. This results in objects below the horizon being projected within sight of the observer at sea level.

Sound, too, plays strange pranks in the North. It carries over much greater distances, especially when temperatures hover around 60° below zero. The barking of dogs can be heard at a distance of ten to twelve miles. An ordinary conversation is heard clearly at half a mile.

To understand the Arctic, we have to understand ice. That seems simple enough until we realize that there are many kinds of ice, sometimes behaving in weird and wonderful ways.

Many a traveler has gasped in amazement on seeing an iceberg for the first time. An iceberg is a block of ice

The Eskimo is well protected by his caribou parka.

that has broken off from a glacier. These floating mountains of ice may be many miles long. Often they tower above the sea for a thousand feet. The part of an iceberg below water is about seven times larger than the part above. This is because an iceberg is made of fresh-water ice, which weighs about seven-eighths as much as sea water.

In the early spring, majestic processions of these floating icebergs—some large and some small—begin their journey southward. By April, May or June, they have reached the northern Atlantic steamer routes. International weather ships are on the lookout and send out warnings as to their location.

A glacier forms from snow packed so solidly that it becomes ice. The largest glaciers, called icecaps, cover plateaus or mountain regions. The interior of Greenland is covered by an icecap thousands of feet deep. Only the Antarctic Icecap is larger than that of Greenland.

Frequently the weight of so much snow and ice will start a portion moving down a mountain or valley. This mass of moving ice, or glacier, pushes slowly ahead like a great frozen river that travels only a few inches a day. When the glacier reaches the sea, its

Only one-eighth of an iceberg shows above water.

edges break off into the icebergs that are so breathtaking.

The ice of the open Polar seas forms slowly. In September, when the sea has been quite still for some days, the surface begins to take on a greasy appearance. This is the first indication of freezing. By the time the water has cooled to about 28.6° F., ice crystals form. These tiny crystals are shaped like small discs, grouped in short columns. They keep increasing until the sea is covered with a mush of crystals. This

All About the Arctic and Antarctic

is known as slush ice, which has the consistency of cooked oatmeal. Soon larger lumps form in it, growing constantly, until they join to form huge, irregularly-shaped fields of ice. Unless broken up by wind or tide, this ice cover increases rapidly in thickness, to a depth of four or five inches within the first forty-eight hours. Thereafter the growth is slower.

In the heart of the Polar Basin, new ice seldom becomes more than six to nine feet thick in the course of one year. Only over a period of some years does it reach a thickness of fifteen or more feet.

With the rise and fall of the tides and the heaving of the sea, the young ice cracks. These cracks widen and close with the movement of the waves. Sea ice is forever forming, freezing, breaking apart, colliding with the thundering roar of heavy cannon.

Almost any vessel can cut through drift ice or loose pack with safety, but an ordinary iron or steel ship runs great danger when the ice floes are closely packed and moving rapidly. Safety for a ship caught in such ice depends on her ability to rise under pressure. In other words the ice, meeting below the hull, lifts the ship up out of the water. It is the heavy pack ice that closes the Polar seas to navigation.

Weather, Wind, Ice and Permafrost

The same bitter cold that freezes Arctic waters freezes the ground to a great depth. It becomes as hard as granite. In fact, the ground of the Arctic region is perpetually frozen except for a few feet of soil at the surface which thaws in the summer.

This permanently frozen ground of the Arctic is known as permafrost. It underlies all Arctic regions, but its depth varies greatly. At Resolute Bay, on Cornwallis Island, permafrost goes down 1,300 feet.

Above such frozen ground, soil temperatures can never be very high. Water is unable to seep down and penetrate that rocklike, frozen soil. It drains off in streams and rivers, or forms the vast shallow bogs of the tundra. During the short Arctic summer, the top layer of the earth thaws and softens. But try to dig a hole, and within minutes your shovel will ring against the stone-hard frozen ground underneath.

Permafrost affects almost every enterprise in the North. When it thaws (as it sometimes does under a building which generates heat in the soil), the character of the ground changes completely. It shrinks and turns into mush, or expands and cracks wide open. Under the constant heaving and lowering of the ground's surface, the only buildings that remain erect for long are those built on stilts or pilings, or on platforms with ventilation between the floor and the frozen earth.

When the first airstrips and roads were being constructed in the Arctic, bulldozers tore away the insulating blanket of mosses which covered ground that had been frozen for thousands of years. The result was chaos, for the suddenly thawed ground heaved and cracked wide open. Today's engineers have learned to leave this natural insulation undisturbed. The permafrost beneath will remain as solid as bed rock.

In recent years there are many signs to prove that the Arctic is slowly melting. This is shown by the rise of average temperatures, by the distribution of the pack ice, and by the recession of glaciers in Norway, Spitsbergen and Greenland. In northern Finland the vegetation period is now from ten to fourteen days longer than it was twenty years ago. This is of tremendous importance in the Far North, where every hour of sunlight counts.

But the great pack ice still remains a formidable barrier. For ages to come it will claim victims among the ships, planes, and men who face up to its challenge.

3.

Arctic Spring and Summer

When spring comes to the Arctic, a miracle occurs. The sun returns to brighten a world long in darkness. With its return, a great thaw begins. Snow melts on the ice, forming vast shallow pools and lakes. The frozen floes of the sea break apart, drifting away in open lanes created by wind and current.

At the first welcome sign of spring, the Eskimos emerge from their damp sod-and-wood houses, or from their snow igloos. They pitch the caribou hide (or canvas) tents in which they will pass the warm months. Everyone is happy. There is a holiday feeling in the

All About the Arctic and Antarctic

air. Children play like puppies. Now there is no night, so boys and girls sleep when they are tired, eat when they are hungry. Throughout the long daylight hours they chase birds or trap foxes. Often, stretched full-length on the sea ice, they jig for fish with a bent pin on a line. Frequently they are rewarded by catching in this fashion the ugly little fish known as sticklebacks. The Eskimo dogs, usually so quick to pick a fight, doze peacefully in the warm sunlight.

To the people of the Northland, this is the best season of the year. True, the meat caches are empty of supplies. But that doesn't matter. Already thousands of seals are emerging from their holes in the ice. Soon there will be more food than the hungriest man and his family can eat.

From the middle of May the sun does not set below the horizon. It circles endlessly in the sky. Gratefully the thawing land soaks up the warmth. By this time the sea ice is covered by a film of water. On land, snow slides magically away from the rocky slopes. Along the shore the hard-packed drifts grow wet and sticky. Melting snow forms the first of the June freshets which swell into the thundering streams of July. That sound of tumbling water, racing down to the sea, is welcome to ears so long accustomed to the silence of

When summer comes, thousands of birds return from the South.

winter. Thousands of little mouselike rodents called lemmings are driven from their burrows by the floods. They cluster on the rocks for safety, only to be snatched up by hawks and owls.

With the approach of warmer weather, the migratory birds reappear. Some have spent the winter months in places as far south as Louisiana or Florida. Others have sought warmth in distant islands of the South Pacific Ocean.

To the Eskimos, the Indians, traders and trappers, the return of the birds is almost as important as the

All About the Arctic and Antarctic

return of the sun. For now there will be eggs to eat! Raw or boiled, it doesn't matter. During the long winter people of the Arctic have had an unbroken diet of meat and fish so eggs are eagerly looked forward to. Those of the snow geese are first in preference, but the eggs of that razor-billed diver, the murre, come in a close second. According to the white man's law, egg gathering is forbidden. But the easygoing Eskimo cheerfully assumes that the white man's laws are made for white men, and he might as well gobble up the precious eggs before the foxes devour them.

With the returning sun, the first flowers burst into bloom. Their rapid development is almost explosive. Some thrust up through the melting snow, impatient for warmth. Others appear in puddles of water among the rocks.

Arctic flowers and plants grow almost everywhere except on or near the glacial ice. But abundant though they are, they are not haphazard in growth. They flourish only in areas best suited to their needs.

Among the rocks of the wide river valleys, purple saxifrage glows against its dull background. On windswept plateaus the yellow Arctic poppy dances wildly in the breeze from the North. Cotton grass borders

Meadows are bright with poppies, harebells and buttercups.

the shallow lakes so abundantly that from a distance it looks like a heavy drift of snow. Meadows brighten with buttercups, with violet cuckoo flowers, with the delicate harebell. It is difficult to believe that only one or two feet below the flowering surface, the scanty soil remains frozen even in the height of summer.

No Arctic plants are poisonous. None has thorns. Because the warm season is so short, few annuals have time to complete their life cycle. So most plants are perennials, blooming year after year. Buds often spend the winter wrapped in a downy cocoon that insulates them against the cold.

All About the Arctic and Antarctic

How, you may ask, is it possible to grow crops in a region where the sun never shines for months at a time? Well, it *is* possible. The Arctic soil has advantages unknown to farmers in more temperate zones: there are no ground blights, no crop diseases. The earth itself has not been worked out by constant planting. In some places it is as richly fertile as the Soviet's black loam region.

As we have seen, during the short summer of continuous daylight, the thermometer often soars to the eighties. Under such conditions two or three crops of hay, as well as other types of farm produce, can be raised. Two hundred miles north of the Arctic Circle, cabbages weighing twenty to thirty pounds are not uncommon. Some have been recorded weighing as much as forty pounds. Vegetables have been raised successfully on the very shores of the Arctic Sea. Potatoes the size of hens' eggs grow in ground that is frozen beyond a depth of six inches. Agricultural scientists have developed a variety of wheat which may be sown farther north than anyone would have thought possible twenty years ago.

It is becoming increasingly apparent that agriculture and market gardening are possible in the North on a scale sufficient to support permanent populations. Some

Arctic Spring and Summer

settlers have demonstrated this by raising as many as twenty different kinds of vegetables and cereals. Even stock farming can be operated successfully where a hot summer sun provides sufficient hay to support cattle throughout the winter months. Domestic animals, bred in more temperate zones, can survive the intense cold if suitably sheltered. Stefansson once predicted that the vast Arctic prairies would provide the future source of the world's meat supply, with millions of reindeer and musk oxen fattening on the coarse grass.

During April, May and June, Northland people are tireless hunters of the seal. They travel great distances over the ice with their dogsleds. Only a few years ago Eskimos used primitive arrows and harpoons in their hunt. Now these have been replaced largely by such modern weapons as rifles of 30.30 caliber, or even the small-bore .22. Frequently the hunter stalks his prey from behind a white screen—a sort of portable blind, made from a square of cloth stretched tight over a frame. To the seal it resembles a piece of moving ice, and the animal's great curiosity is usually its undoing.

As the weather grows warmer, the rise and fall of the tide break the ice away from the land. Cracks widen into lanes of open water. These stretch for many miles through the thick sea ice. It is along such lanes that the

Often seals lie basking in the sun beside cracks in the ice.

seals emerge in great numbers. Sometimes they frolic like puppies or perhaps just lie basking in the warm sun.

Often in the never-ending search for food, the hunters are forced to be away from home for days. At such

Arctic Spring and Summer

times they live entirely off the products of the sea. Almost always seal meat is eaten raw or very lightly boiled. What cannot be consumed is cached on shore. And if the summer's warmth should spoil the meat, what matter? Eskimos look upon tainted meat or fish as a special delicacy.

By mid-July the land is almost free of snow. Only in shaded gullies does it linger. But the mountain ranges still dazzle the eye with their eternal icecaps and snow fields. Now the sun shines all day long out of a bright blue sky. It shines all night too. At noon it lies due south, at midnight due north. Instead of setting, it remains in full view, though low in the sky.

Welcome though the summer is to dwellers of the Northland, it presents one tremendous problem. Out of the bogs that form when the topsoil thaws, swarm great hordes of mosquitoes and flies. All winter long insect eggs and caterpillars were frozen until they were as hard as the ice in which they lay encased. But with summer's return a new generation of insects is born. Between spring and fall they are the curse of the North.

Only on hilltops in a brisk wind, may you be free of these pests. In the valleys they rise up from the ground in clouds. They invade your nostrils, your eyes and ears, your mouth. Stefansson records that in the early days of Canada's fur trade, the trappers found the insects more of a trial than the knee-deep mud through which the men had to carry their heavy packs.

Caribou are often driven frantic by the stinging swarms of insects. Dogs are sometimes so badly bitten that their eyes swell shut. Some animals are even stung to death. In the settlements, the sunny wall of a white house appears black with a mass of mosquitoes. Often the insects gather so thickly on windows that it is impossible to see through the glass. Scientists are seeking some effective means of insect control; but so far the immensity of the land has made the task all but hopeless. Bumblebees, butterflies and bluebottles add to the insect horde.

By mid-July the sea ice has melted so that it is unsafe for hunting with dogsled. Now the Eskimos take to their big skin-covered boats called *umiaks*. In open water they hunt day after day. Hundreds and hundreds of seals are killed, for the storage places must be stocked with meat and blubber against the lean months of the winter so soon to come.

The approach of autumn is the most important season for the Eskimos of the Eastern Arctic. This is the time

By mid-July Eskimo hunters go to sea in big skin-covered boats.

when the seals are so fat that they float after being killed. Few are lost.

It seems incredible that small groups of Eskimos can devour the tremendous number of animals that are slaughtered each year. But one Eskimo eats five or six pounds of meat at a single meal; and it must be remembered that the dogs also must be fed. One Husky requires as much food as a man.

As summer draws to an end, the sun dips below the northern horizon for the first time in three months. Each day thereafter it sets a little earlier and farther to

All About the Arctic and Antarctic

the west, and rises a little later, farther to the east. Gradually the land undergoes a change. At night puddles of water freeze over. Morning finds the soil frost-bitten and hard. Hilltops glisten with the first snowfall, then turn brown again as the lingering sun devours it. Flowers which have been frost-nipped during the night revive miraculously under the day's warmth.

By this time the migratory birds are preparing to depart. Their young have matured or have fallen prey to their natural enemies. The air is filled with the sound of bird cries and beating wings. Above the tumult, wild and free rises the honking of the snow geese.

And then one day all these sounds have ceased. The birds have headed south. Only the raven, the snowy owl, the ptarmigan and the gerfalcon remain. By this time nearly every beast of the tundra has put on its white winter dress. White fur is almost invisible against a background of snow. So the animals of the Far North protect themselves by changing their dark summer coats to white. The little lemming, however, remains brown, for he will spend the white months in his burrow under the snow. The raven, bold and obstinate as he is, remains glossy black in a world of whiteness.

A hush falls over the Northland, as if it were holding its breath, waiting again for winter's darkness to fall.

4.

The Long Winter Night

Winter conditions vary greatly in different parts of the Far North; but the pattern of the long winter night is much the same, wherever you live north of the Arctic Circle.

Let's suppose you happen to be spending the winter on north Baffin Island in the Canadian Arctic. During the intense cold of late October and early November, you will see bays and rivers freezing over. You will watch ice forming on the open sea. Day after day the hours of sunlight become shorter. Soon the sun will have vanished behind the hills in the south. Strong winds come roaring in out of the north.

All About the Arctic and Antarctic

Hunting on the sea in open boats has become difficult and dangerous. The big skin-covered *umiaks* are hauled ashore. Their short travel season is over for another year. The Eskimos are growing impatient for the ice to grow thick enough for them to roam far and wide over the frozen surface of the sea.

New ice is forming slowly on the open water. It spreads out in all directions, like a gigantic lid being pressed down over the restless surface of the sea. With each advance and recession of the tides, the shore ice thickens. Gradually it extends farther and farther out into the slow-freezing sea.

At night, displays of the aurora borealis are becoming more brilliant and more frequent. The mysterious bands of light flicker and shift, glow and grow dim—pale yellow, delicate pink or lilac. The stars shine with a hard, bright glitter in the dark sky.

So far, in the intense cold, little snow has fallen on the ice of north Baffin. This is a blessing for the hunter, since it enables him to locate easily the breathing holes of the seals. Such holes are about a foot in diameter. Frequently they are rimmed with glass-ice that forms as the animals push water up ahead of them to reach the surface. No matter how freezing the cold, the seals will keep these holes open throughout the winter.

The hunter waits, spear in hand, by the breathing hole of a seal.

Twice a month, when the tides are at their highest, the ice cover shifts under the pressures of the tides. Long cracks appear in the sea ice. Often these cracks run for miles, cutting lanes through the ice cover. The open water quickly freezes over, but not before the seals have discovered this new means of access to open air. Sometimes they abandon their old breathing holes in the thick ice to form a whole new line in the fresh ice.

For the hunters, this is a time of furious activity. The caches must be filled with enough meat and blubber to nourish a man and his family and his dogs throughout the long winter. There will be many days after the sun vanishes, days of storm, when it will be impossible to hunt. Now there is no time to be lost. As many seals as possible must be killed, for by the first of November the trapping season will begin. Then all of a man's waking hours must be devoted to following the trap line.

From November to March, the pursuit of the Arctic fox is the main activity of the trapper. This means many miles of travel by dogsled, often in almost total darkness. Now is the time when the Eskimo builds the snow igloo for which he is famous. He builds it solely as a shelter to be used when he is hunting far from home.

It is exciting to watch an igloo being built. The Eskimo has only his knowledge and skill to help him, his knife, and the snow around him. He chooses a deep snowdrift that has formed during a single storm. Blocks cut from many-layered drifts have a tendency to break.

An igloo is built as a shelter for hunters far from home.

Neat slabs are cut, about three feet long, two feet high, and eight inches thick. When one block has been cut from the snowdrift, the other blocks come out more easily. Soon a dozen or more such slabs of snow form a circle in the trench where our Eskimo stands.

The builder works rapidly. A low dome begins to rise, the walls sloping strongly inward. They are kept from falling by the snow packed into the seams. The Eskimo cements his blocks together just as a stone mason works with bricks. Working from the inside, the builder literally builds himself into his home. When the igloo is completed, he must cut an opening in order to get out. The size of the igloo depends of course on the number of hunters. A snow house fifteen feet in diameter is considered a large one.

The test of the workman's skill comes in fitting the topmost, key block. To accomplish this, the builder crawls outside for a moment and places a block on the unfinished dome. Then returning to the inside, he reaches up through the opening and eases the block toward him. He whittles it down to proper size, slides it into place, fills in the chinks with snow. There, the igloo is finished! The whole job has been accomplished within forty minutes.

Although made of snow, an igloo is snug and warm inside.

A platform of snow is now built across one end of the interior. Caribou skins and robes are placed on this to make a sleeping shelf. A shallow basin of seal oil is prepared for fuel. In this a wick of dry reindeer moss is set aflame. In no time the igloo is snug and warm. The weary hunters are wolfing down their evening meal.

By the first week in December the sun has set on north Baffin for the last time. Thereafter, a faint glow

All About the Arctic and Antarctic

of light appears in the south each morning at about ten-thirty. Noon is like dawn. The glow has vanished by half past one or two. By the middle of December, even this pale noonday light has faded to dusk. If there should be an overcast in the sky, then for twenty-four hours around the clock it will be as dark as midnight.

This condition prevails throughout January, when gradually the long winter night begins to retreat. First light now comes a little earlier each morning, lingers on longer beyond noon. The sky overhead reflects a warm glow from the still invisible sun.

By the end of January, pale colors begin to tint the land. Delicate pinks and golds paint the high clouds, reflect downward to touch every pinnacle of ice. Long blue shadows reach out across the pink of the snow-covered land. To the north, stars glitter in a sky of deepest blue.

This gradual return of light alters the pattern of daily living on north Baffin. Hours of sleeping again conform to hours of light and dark. Less time is needed to look after the trap lines, for light makes it possible for a hunter to travel faster and farther each day.

As February comes to an end, the stars are snuffed out by the encroaching light. High in the sky, the tre-

The Long Winter Night

mendous shadow cast by the mass of the earth can be seen rushing through space. Suddenly, like a herald of good tidings, a shaft of rosy light shoots straight up into the heavens. Another follows, then another. The entire sky is ablaze. And then miraculously over the rim of the southern horizon, the blood-red disk of the sun slides into view. Daylight has returned again to north Baffin.

The long winter night is over.

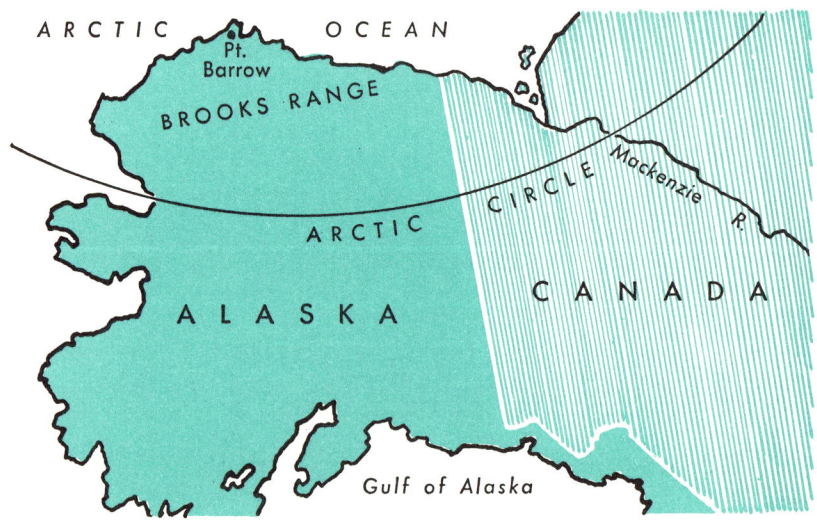

5.

The Treasure Chest of the Arctic

Throughout the Arctic there are vast natural resources. Most of these are essential to our modern way of life. This is particularly true of our own Territory of Alaska. Actually, only a third of this great Territory lies within the Arctic Circle, but its potential wealth barely has been tapped.

In 1867 the United States purchased Alaska from Russia for $7,200,000—or two cents per acre. This purchase was the greatest bargain in the history of the United States. Since then, the gold mines of Alaska have yielded more than fifty times the original cost of the Territory. And today the copper output exceeds in value that of gold.

The Treasure Chest of the Arctic

A hundred years ago, oil was discovered near Point Barrow, the northern extremity of the coast. In 1943 a serious fuel shortage in California stimulated active oil production which is going on in the Territory today. Oil seepages in many places along the Arctic shore hint at hidden lakes of oil still to be uncovered.

In the past few years, interest has been shown in prospecting areas in the Brooks Range. These great mountains divide the center of Arctic Alaska. Samples of rare minerals have been found there, as well as seepages of oil. The Government appropriates funds to help prospectors who will work faithfully and report their findings.

It is in the Brooks Range area that Naval Petroleum Reserve No. 4 was established in 1923. This comprises 37,000 square miles north of the Arctic Circle. All phases of exploratory work are being carried out there.

Veins of coal, possibly as great in extent as Pennsylvania's original supply, are as yet unmined. It is possible that Alaska may one day be producing coal when Pennsylvania, Kentucky and Illinois are scraping the bottom of the bin.

Valuable deposits of tungsten, bismuth, antimony, gypsum, tin, lead and silver have been found in Alaska too. Virtually all the platinum mined in America comes from one small sector in northeastern Alaska.

All About the Arctic and Antarctic

One of the most interesting discoveries of recent times was the rich deposit of jade found in the Shungnak area of the Arctic. Jade was formerly thought to be an exclusive product of southern China. Alaskan jade is of excellent quality and is being used for bearings in airplanes as well as for jewelry.

The Arctic Circle Exploration Company, responsible for discovering the jade deposits, also found large quantities of tremolite asbestos. This is used as a filtering agent for blood plasma. At the time of the discovery, the supply in the United States was almost exhausted.

Alaska's icy waters teem with fish. Canning and processing the catch are the Territory's principal industry. The value of products annually prepared for market averages around $100,000,000. This forms the background of Alaska's wealth.

Five species of Pacific salmon exist, all occurring in commercial quantities. The largest of these is the king salmon, known also as the Chinook. Often it weighs as much as twenty pounds. In Bristol Bay alone, during the short run of the fishing season, $12,000,000 worth of salmon is the average yearly catch. Cod, herring and halibut are also caught.

In some parts of Alaska, magnificent trees clothe the

The Treasure Chest of the Arctic

land. There you will see towering Sitka spruce, birch, black cottonwood, cedars, hemlock, aspen and larch. In many places, for mile upon mile, the ring of an ax against timber has never been heard. These mighty forests occupy over sixty per cent of the land area of the Territory. For many years to come they can supply much of the pulp needed for newsprint in all parts of the United States.

As you move north in Alaska, there is no sharp line to mark where tree growth ends and the true Arctic begins. For in sheltered bends of the rivers, tall and graceful trees often are found growing far beyond the normal tree line. The cottonwood and the white spruce grow farther north than any other big trees. Beyond the last of these, you will find no others until you have crossed the Polar Basin and reached a corresponding climate on the Siberian side. It is these trees that supply lumber for building the northernmost settlements.

An Arctic settlement may be only a huddle of half a dozen crude houses, or it may be many times that number. But whatever its size, it is the place where Eskimo and trapper come to trade their pelts and to buy supplies from the general store. It is where men and women go to church, children to school. It is the place

An Arctic settlement may be only a handful of houses.

of administration in the land. It is where the doctor, the dentist and the missionary pause briefly on their lonely rounds.

More than anything else today, the Territory of Alaska needs settlers—solid citizens who will come and work and stay. Homesteaders may acquire up to 160 acres of land by living on it for three years. They must build a house and bring at least one-sixteenth of the area under cultivation within two years and a total of one-eighth by the end of the third year.

The Treasure Chest of the Arctic

Arctic Alaska is one of the world's last and most exciting frontiers. But Canada controls the largest percentage of all the Arctic lands.

Canada's Northwest Territories alone are so huge that they are divided into three districts. The first is Mackenzie, the most productive, and through which the great river of the same name flows. The second is Keewatin, which lies between Mackenzie and Hudson Bay. Keewatin consists largely of unpopulated tundra. The third is Franklin, which embraces most of the islands of the Arctic Archipelago. These lands cover more than 1,500,000 square miles.

Canada receives rich returns from her part of the Arctic: supplies of nickel, lead, silver, copper, coal, iron, uranium and gold.

The little gold-mining town called Yellowknife now boasts an airport, hotels, restaurants, electricity—all made possible by the precious metal buried deep in the ground.

Oil was first produced in Norman Wells about 1920. Scores of enormous tanks, in which the fuel is stored, line the river. During World War II a pipe line was laid westward to Whitehorse, a distance of almost 600 miles. By such means gasoline could be furnished for

The Canadian part of the Arctic is rich in oil.

trucks using the Alaska Highway, as well as for airplane use in Alaska and at Pacific coast ports.

One of the greatest sources of radioactive minerals is at Port Radium on Great Bear Lake. The discovery which led eventually to this development is credited to a man named Gilbert LaBine. At the age of fourteen, LaBine had worked in the mines at Cobalt, Ontario. At fifteen, on his own, the boy had staked out a silver claim of considerable value. Years later, on a flight across the Great Bear Lake country, the man's practiced eye spotted on a cliff at the lake's edge colorations suggesting great mineral wealth.

The Treasure Chest of the Arctic

The following winter LaBine returned to the region. Eagerly he applied his pick to the face of the rock wall bordering the lake. Before the day's end, he had found thirty-eight distinct minerals. Among them were cobalt, bismuth, and a wide vein of silver. One of the minerals, however, was more important than all the others put together—pitchblende. This is the ore from which radium and uranium are refined. LaBine was one of the few men in Canada at that time who could have recognized the blue-gray rock for what it was. This was the first time pitchblende had been discovered in the Western Hemisphere. In LaBine's hand lay the beginnings of the atomic bomb that later exploded over Hiroshima. In fact that very bomb contained uranium which came from LaBine's cliff on the shores of Echo Bay, Great Bear Lake.

In Labrador great wealth is being uncovered constantly. The Labrador Peninsula (the world's third largest) is a tremendous rocky plateau. Along its eastern and southern coasts are towering mountain ranges. The rest is a harsh land of rushing rivers and muskeg, the latter being a thick black mud. There are many lakes, innumerable waterfalls, deep gorges. In temperature, Labrador is almost wholly Arctic. It has only one frost-free month—July. Northwest winds howl over plain and valley, often at sixty miles per hour. Locked within this wild terrain, a tremendous iron deposit has lain untouched for half a billion years.

A Frenchman named Jacques Cartier was Labrador's discoverer. For four centuries after Cartier, the great Peninsula resisted all efforts to mine its treasures. Only since World War II has the true extent of its wealth begun to be explored.

Canada's newest railway, completed in 1954, knifes its way across Labrador's high plateau for 369 miles. It connects the iron country with the sea. Master engineers designed a tunnel to bore through the 3,000-foot granite barrier which walls off the interior of the peninsula. Only the promised riches of the Labrador-Ungava iron country could have forced so bold a venture. The total cost was $235,000,000. To keep the railway-builders supplied, everything from nails to tractors had to be flown into the country. At the peak of activities, seventy-five pilots were employed, and planes took off at the rate of one every five minutes.

At the new town called Knob Lake, in Labrador, the face of the red crater is being gouged up in ten-ton gulps. Diesel trucks, loaded to capacity, strain up the inclines to send the precious iron ore on the first stage

In Labrador iron ore is gouged out in ten-ton gulps.

of its journey to the steel mills of the United States. The ore moves at the rate of 10,000,000 tons a year. When the St. Lawrence Seaway is completed, this figure will probably be doubled.

Rich copper deposits are being uncovered near Chimo, the old Hudson's Bay Company post on Ungava Bay. There is still another resource in Labrador: due to

All About the Arctic and Antarctic

the harsh climate, tree growth is exceedingly slow. Consequently the growth rings of the trees are so close together as to be almost indistinguishable, and this has offered a surprising by-product. Paper makers are clamoring for the long fiber in the pulpwood, which turns into superb paper. In the rocklands of Labrador, great acres of spruces are waiting to be harvested for this purpose.

From the innumerable lakes and rivers of the peninsula, as much as 12,000,000 horsepower may some day be derived—almost five times that produced by our Grand Coulee dam. It is estimated that Grand Falls, on the Hamilton River, can be harnessed to produce 4,000,000 horsepower of its own.

From Spitsbergen (an island within the Arctic Circle) Norway mines a large proportion of its coal—coal of the finest quality. For a considerable part of the year the Gulf Stream keeps this island's west coast clear of ice. This means that coal can be shipped out during four or five months of fair weather. The 3,000 miners who are responsible for producing it live under severest Arctic conditions. In almost complete isolation they endure four months of winter darkness, with temperatures dropping to 40° below zero.

Greenland represents practically all varieties of Arc-

The Treasure Chest of the Arctic

tic conditions. Its northern extremity, Peary Land, is the part of our earth closest to the North Pole. Its southernmost point, Cape Farewell, has the same latitude as Oslo, Norway.

Southwest Greenland is the only place on earth where cryolite is mined in quantities of practical importance. Cryolite is a rare mineral necessary to the production of aluminum. Only two other sources of it are known. One of these is at Pike's Peak, Colorado. The other is at Miass, in the Urals. In both of these places, however, the quantity of the mineral is small, the quality poor. From time to time, rumors have leaked from behind the Iron Curtain concerning a Russian cryolite mine in active operation in East Siberia. We do not know for sure whether this is fact or fiction.

Cryolite is one of the most important assets in Greenland. Most of the profits from it go directly to the administration of the island—to the trade, social welfare, medical care, and education of the native population. About one-third of this valuable mineral is purchased by Canada and the United States.

Last but not least, the now-extinct mammoth is of considerable importance in the Arctic. A species of elephant, with huge in-curving tusks and shaggy coat, the mammoth once ranged far and wide over Siberia, Europe, and northern North America. Ancient cave drawings prepared modern scientists somewhat for the discovery of tusks and skeletons, even of whole beasts, preserved in the frozen soil of the North.

This "fossil ivory" is of great value to the natives of Alaska, where it is still found. From it they fashion innumerable objects. Eskimos are clever artisans, and their wonderful ivory carvings are recognized as folk art of a high order.

Truly the Arctic regions are among the treasure chests of the world!

Fossilized mammoth tusks are often found in the Arctic.

6.

Fur-Bearers of the North

Nanook is the Eskimo name for the white polar bear. This animal is the undisputed king of the Northland. Wherever seals gather on the pack ice, Nanook is there to hunt them down. The polar bear is really a sea mammal, seldom found far from sea ice.

During the greater part of the year, Nanook is constantly on the move. One of his main routes runs from King Charles Island and Greenland to Spitsbergen; but he is found everywhere in the Arctic where seals are plentiful. In habit Nanook follows the light. He moves south in the fall, heads north again in the spring. Occasionally he has been seen in the central Polar Basin, as

All About the Arctic and Antarctic

far north as 88°. An immensely powerful swimmer, the polar bear is capable of swimming several hundred miles if necessary. Although he weighs as much as a thousand pounds when full grown, this seemingly clumsy animal is agile and quick-moving.

Nanook is also exceedingly clever in stalking his prey. There is no end to his patience when hunting. An inch at a time he eases his great body over the ice toward a dozing seal. Frequently he covers the tip of his black nose with one white paw and thus is less easily seen against the snow. When the seal is within reach, the bear hurls himself forward, crushing his victim's skull with a single blow.

The polar bear is a solitary animal. Only in spring are the male and female seen together. Bear cubs are born late in winter. Their home is a burrow in the snow. At birth a cub is scarcely larger than a full-grown rat. It is blind and almost without fur. But the female bear is a devoted mother, feeding her cubs, sheltering them from wind and storm. The cubs remain with their mother for the first two years of their life. Then they set out on their own solitary wanderings.

Ordinarily the polar bear avoids a man; but this is not always so by any means. A female protecting her

A mother polar bear will fight valiantly for her cubs.

cubs is invariably dangerous. Eskimos have hunted down bears ruthlessly for their meat and fur. Every part of the animal is considered edible except the liver, which is poisonous. The Eskimo takes great care to dispose of the liver when a kill is made, so that his dogs will not eat it and become poisoned.

The clever Arctic fox follows in the wake of Nanook. Keeping well out of reach of the bear's punishing

All About the Arctic and Antarctic

claws, he devours any scraps of food that the larger animal has left behind.

There are two varieties of this little animal: the so-called blue fox, whose coat is not blue at all, but a handsome smoky gray; and the true Arctic fox, whose mottled yellowish-brown summer coat turns snow-white in winter. The livelihood of the natives of the eastern Arctic is based on the white fox. Sale of the skins to the Hudson's Bay Company provides the bulk of the money for the year ahead. The snowy pelts are in great demand in all the fur markets of the world.

The clever little fox is often seen hundreds of miles from land, tripping lightly over the pack ice. In summer he dines well at the bird rookeries, killing and eating birds and their eggs. But the fox has enemies of his own, principally man. So relentlessly has he been hunted

The fox's yellowish-brown summer coat turns white in winter.

Fur-Bearers of the North

down for his handsome winter coat that in some areas (notably Spitsbergen) the bark of the animal is now seldom heard.

But if the fox is one of the cleverest of Arctic creatures, the musk ox is one of the stupidest. It is, however, perhaps the world's hardiest animal. The musk ox seems to be a leftover from some prehistoric age. Scientists have given the beast the name *ovibos,* which means sheep-cow. And that is what the animal seems to be: a

Musk oxen stand in a circle to protect themselves from a wolf.

sort of cow with a coat of wool. It also has a hairy mane, sheeplike teeth, a cow's tongue and heavy horns. The musk ox can resist any temperature, high or low. It thrives on dwarf willows and grasses, in winter pawing away the snow to get at its food.

The musk ox has developed a perfect defense against the Arctic wolf. When attacked, the group forms a circle. With the largest animals on the outside, they stand shoulder to shoulder with lowered heads. A blow from their powerful horns or sharp hoofs can be fatal. But one of their greatest protections is the heavy wool around their neck; this fills a wolf's mouth and prevents his teeth from doing harm.

The meat of the musk ox compares to the finest Grade-A beef. For this reason, the whalemen of the nineteenth century slaughtered the animals by the thousands. It is estimated that there are now only a few hundred left on the North American mainland, with perhaps another 35,000 scattered along the east coast of Greenland and some of the Arctic islands. They are extinct in Europe and Asia. Fortunately musk oxen are protected today by law. The wolf is its only remaining enemy.

The typical Arctic wolf is a light, tawny yellow,

The tawny yellow Arctic wolf preys on caribou or reindeer.

with a few dark hairs running down the back. Eskimos maintain that light wolves are old wolves; but dark females occasionally have been seen with pure white cubs. The Arctic wolf enjoys the evil reputation common to all wolves. A crafty animal, it preys on caribou or reindeer, on smaller beasts, even on birds. The wolf is the plague of the Northern hunter, for he robs traps whenever possible, seldom stepping into one himself. He is also an enemy of the sled dog, being strong enough to make off with a dog that weighs almost as much as he

All About the Arctic and Antarctic

does. In spite of the fact that he can run faster than any other northern animal, the Arctic wolf is extremely wary. A strange scent (that of a man, for example) will send him loping away.

Contrary to popular belief, wolves do not travel in packs. Seldom are more than six or eight of them seen together. Most of the time they hunt singly or in pairs. With the exception of the polar bear (to whom they give a wide berth) they will eat practically anything.

Leaves and shoots are the favorite food of the white hare.

Fur-Bearers of the North

But the white Arctic hare is one of their favorite tidbits.

The white hare is widespread in the Canadian Arctic and Greenland. This beautiful little animal is about the size of a fox terrier and has liquid brown eyes. It feeds largely on young leaves and shoots. Where the vegetation is rich, the hare is found in large flocks. The great speed of the little hare was once its protection, but that was in the days before firearms. The skin of the polar hare is so fragile that it is used only when nothing stronger can be found. Eskimos sometimes use it to line their boots.

An animal considerably smaller than the hare is the little lemming. This is a weasel-like creature that hibernates in the winter, digging deep burrows in the snow. Its special foes are hawks and owls. It is so difficult to capture, and its beautiful pelt so fragile and hard to match, that the people who set styles in the great cities of the world have never tried to make the lemming fashionable.

Let us turn from this smallest of Arctic animals to one of the largest—the caribou. The caribou is much the same size and color as the American moose; but his enormous, branching antlers are much larger. Both male and female have such antlers, shedding them once a year.

Clothing and blankets are made from caribou skin.

Each spring, before the first thaws melt the surface snow, herds of caribou emerge from the forests where they have wintered and head north across the barren tundra. The cows and yearlings lead the way. The bulls straggle a day or two behind. Moving ever northward, across rivers and lakes, they press on to the very shores of the Polar Sea. There the calves are born.

Fur-Bearers of the North

By this time their coats are thin and fly-bitten, for this is the shedding season and the season of the plague of flies. The warble fly in particular makes the caribou's life miserable.

As soon as the calves are strong enough to travel, the herd starts slowly back toward the forests far in the south. Now the bulls lead the way, protecting the calves from wolves. The herd reaches the tree line early in November and re-enters the sanctuary of the forests.

The caribou fully deserves to have his likeness on the back of the Canadian twenty-five-cent piece. Without this animal, great stretches of the North would be uninhabitable. It has sometimes been called a walking department store. And this is why: caribou fur provides clothing, sleeping bags, shoes and blankets. The scraped skins are turned into dog harnesses, tents, buckets, and *kayaks* (the Eskimo boats). Sinews are transformed into lashings, thread, harpoon lines. Bones and antlers become tools—knives, arrows, thimbles, needles. The bone marrow and fat serve as fuel. Moreover, the entire animal is edible, from the eyes (considered a special Eskimo treat) to the half-digested mosses in the stomach, known as "tundra salad."

Occasionally, for some reason no one knows, the

All About the Arctic and Antarctic

caribou herds alter the course of their yearly migrations. When this occurs, starvation faces the people who are so completely dependent on this valuable animal.

Fortunately the caribou is now protected in some measure by government regulation. But the slaughter in previous years was on a grand scale. David Thompson, a noted explorer of the Northwest Company, once estimated a single herd at 3,500,000 animals. Today the total number of caribous is believed to be a mere 750,000.

The reindeer is a sort of domesticated caribou. It is the only source of fresh meat for the people of Aklavik, in the Mackenzie River delta. There (if you should drop in) a meal of reindeerburgers will cost you $1.65. There are six of these herds now in the Canadian Arctic. Their presence there is one of the epic stories of the North.

The story began in 1935, when the Canadian Government purchased 3,195 reindeer in Alaska. There was a special reason for doing this. The fur harvests of the natives had been seriously cut down by the overuse of firearms. The Government felt that reindeer would help to offset this difficulty.

An old Laplander named Andrew Bahr, with a few

Fur-Bearers of the North

helpers, was entrusted with the heroic task of driving the herd across the top of the continent to its new home.

The drive was expected to occupy a year and a half. Instead, it took six terrible winters. Few of the original animals that started out from Alaska completed the journey. During the first winter, hundreds panicked. They cut loose from the herd and broke for parts unknown. The following winters were among the severest on record in the North. Sometimes the thermometer dropped to 70° below zero. But Bahr and his men could not seek shelter; they had to remain with their charges or lose them. Wolves skulked always on the fringes of the herd, pouncing on any animal that faltered. One terrific storm scattered five hundred of the reindeer, and six months were consumed in rounding them up again. When the herd finally reached the end of its journey, there were 2,300 animals left, most of them having been born on the way.

Today some 8,000 reindeer are being looked after by a number of Eskimo families in the Canadian Arctic. There are a number of sizable herds in Alaska. The Laplanders, too, have succeeded well in domesticating reindeer, and their herds are an important part of the Lapland economy.

All About the Arctic and Antarctic

It is in Canada's Aklavik, also, that the greatest muskrat trapping grounds are to be found. In countless pools strewn over the boggy delta, these little animals swarm by the hundreds of thousands. Children on their way to the mission school have their own trap lines. In 1950, 300,000 muskrat skins were shipped out, each selling for around $2.00. But by 1954 muskrat fur was no longer fashionable in the world's great cities. The price dropped to fifty cents per skin. Today the trapper seems to be faced with an ever diminishing market. He can only hope that one of these days fashions will change again, and once more the little muskrat will be popular for ladies' coats and trimmings.

7.
Creatures of the Arctic Sea

The preponderance of life in the Arctic lies within the sea. Seals come first in importance, perhaps because they fill so many needs of the people who live in the Far North. The meat of the seal is a principal source of food. Oil from the blubber, or fat, becomes fuel. Seal oil, when set afire, maintains a steady flame. Sealskins are made into boots and other articles of clothing. The smooth hide of the bearded seal makes the stoutest soles for boots. The bones become implements or utensils. No part of the animal goes to waste.

The number of seals varies greatly in different parts of the Arctic. Wherever there are strong ocean currents, resulting in broken ice, you will find an abundance of these animals. They are scarcest where the ice is thick and unbroken, since these conditions offer few opportunities for the seal to come up to breathe the air he needs.

There are several types of seals in Arctic waters, but two specimens predominate in the Polar Basin—the bearded seal and the ringed seal.

The ringed seal (so-called because of its markings) prefers living close to the land, where the ice breaks up early in the spring. There he is assured of an abundance of food—herring, polar cod and shellfish. Throughout the winter, ringed seals maintain breathing holes in the ice. As a rule each seal has a series of four or five holes about a mile apart. It is at these vantage points that the hunter stands ready with rifle or harpoon. But the seal has other enemies than man. Polar bears, sharks and killer whales are always on the watch for him.

The bearded seal gets its name from the coarse bristles sprouting from its muzzle. This animal is larger than the ringed seal, averaging some five or six hundred pounds in weight. It reaches a length of nine or ten feet. It is not so apt to maintain breathing holes during the winter, preferring lanes of open water. To the Eskimo the meat of this seal is particularly tasty. Contrary to popular

Where the ice is thin and easily broken, seals are abundant.

All About the Arctic and Antarctic

belief, no seal meat is fishy in flavor. In fact it tastes very much like our own beef, though it is somewhat darker in color.

There is one type of seal found throughout the entire Arctic region. This is known as the hair seal. It has even been sighted in the vicinity of the North Pole. It is much smaller than the bearded seal, averaging around one hundred fifty pounds in weight.

Arctic seal hunting has been an active industry since the early part of the nineteenth century. Today it still brings in substantial financial returns. More than 500,000 animals are killed each year by hunters operating in the main sealing grounds. These are the drift ice east of Greenland, the stormy waters east of Newfoundland, and Labrador. The furs, hides, blubber and oil of the seal bring in many millions of dollars a year.

The Greenland hair seal forms the basis of this industry. The new-born seal has the most valuable fur: the "white coat" and the "blue black." The pelt of the infant seal retains its hair for the first eight or ten days after birth. This is known as "hair-fast." It is essential that the seal hunters reach the main breeding grounds at this time. The new-born animals are unable to swim and lie helpless on the ice. They fall easy

Creatures of the Arctic Sea

victims to the hunters, who sometimes kill thousands in a single day.

The Pribilof Islands (purchased with the Territory of Alaska) are the home of the fabulous fur seals. These animals differ from hair seals in that there is no season when their coat is other than perfect. The Pribilof herds number in millions. The islands themselves were first discovered in 1786 by a Russian navigator named Gerasmin Pribilof. He had heard an ancient Eskimo legend concerning a rocky island north of the Aleutians, where great numbers of fur seals were said to congregate every summer. Believing that most legends have some basis in fact, the Russian decided to look into the matter. By sheer chance he fell in with a migrating herd of seals. He followed them to their breeding grounds and discovered that the legend was a true story.

Since that time, the value in furs taken from those bleak islands amounts to many times the sum originally paid for all Alaska. Each year some 70,000 skins are taken. After the valuable pelt has been removed, oil is extracted from the blubber. The meat itself is a great favorite with the natives of that region. The bones are ground into a meal used in poultry and animal foods. The skins are carefully prepared, then packed

A walrus is very agile in the water, but very awkward on land.

and shipped to the firm in St. Louis, Missouri, which holds the contract for selling them at public auction on our Government's behalf. These skins alone bring in an annual average of $4,000,000.

The walrus, sometimes called a sea horse, was one of the earliest Arctic mammals to be known in Europe. Apart from its great size, the walrus differs from the seal in having two ivory tusks in its upper jaw. These tusks are often two feet in length, and are useful in

Creatures of the Arctic Sea

digging in the mud of the sea floor for clams and mussels. Unlike other members of the seal family, the walrus does not live on fish.

In the water the huge, ungainly body is very agile. On land, however, its movements are slow and awkward. Walrus herds gather in close formation on shore, thus falling easy prey to the hunter. But when wounded, this animal can use its tusks with swift and terrible effect. In battle the bellowing of a walrus is fearsome to hear.

Walrus blubber yields an immense amount of oil, but the animal is valued chiefly for the fine ivory of its tusks. The durable hide also finds a ready market. In the world's big cities this hide goes to make some of the finest and most expensive luggage. For the Eskimo it serves many purposes, principally for the skin covering of the seagoing *umiaks,* or boats. At one time walruses were abundant in all Arctic waters; but, like the great whales, they have been hunted down so relentlessly that today their numbers are greatly reduced.

Several types of whales are found in Arctic waters. The Greenland right whale is a baleen or whalebone type. It is a true ice mammal. Because the curve of

All About the Arctic and Antarctic

its head is arched like a drawn bow, the early hunters called this whale a bowhead. The enormous head takes up one-third of the body, which is known to reach a length of sixty-five feet. It is black in color with flecks of white.

The bowhead lives only in the Arctic Sea, in Hudson Bay, in Greenland waters, and in the Bering and Okhotsk seas. Through the years its numbers have been greatly depleted. It was hunted chiefly for its baleen, or whalebone, which is very fine and pliable. This baleen lines the mouth of the whale and acts as a sort of sieve to strain food from the sea. During the last century, whalebone was used principally to make carriage whips and ladies' dress stays. In those days it sold for five dollars a pound. Since a large whale would produce 3,000 pounds of baleen, a fine profit was assured to the Yankee whaler. But in the course of time a substitute called "featherbone" was invented for making whips and stays. Outfitting expensive whaling voyages was no longer profitable.

The white whale, or beluga, is much smaller than the bowhead. It seldom attains a length of more than twenty feet. The beluga is plentiful along the coast of Alaska, especially in the Bering Sea and the Arctic Ocean. It has even been known to ascend the Yukon

Creatures of the Arctic Sea

River for a considerable distance. Eskimos sometimes make great killings of the white whale by driving them into shallow waters, where they are helpless. A beluga killed in deep water sinks like a stone.

Porpoises and dolphins are found in all oceans. Actually they belong to the family of toothed whales. They are graceful creatures which seem to enjoy company so much that they will spend hours capering under a ship's bows.

But there is nothing playful about the largest member of the porpoise family—the killer whale. This is one

With one bite a killer whale can chop a seal in two.

All About the Arctic and Antarctic

of the most ferocious of living creatures. The killers reach an average length of twenty-five feet and weigh up to fifteen tons. In their upper and lower jaws they have a row of long, wicked teeth. With one bite they can chop a seal or a man in two pieces. From a considerable distance they may be distinguished by a six-foot-high dorsal fin. Hunting in packs, killer whales shoot through the water like living torpedoes. Nothing that swims is safe from their attack. The oceans of the globe are their range, from the Arctic to the Antarctic.

One of the most astonishing of all Arctic sea mammals is the narwhal. Though a member of the porpoise family, it is actually a small whale. When young, the narwhal is slate-colored. This color deepens with age to a mottled black. Like the walrus, the narwhal has two tusks, only one of which is usually visible. This tusk grows out of the left upper jaw—a long spiral of ivory which often reaches a length of eight feet. No one knows how this tusk is used or what purpose it serves. Some people believe that the legend of the unicorn—the horse with a single horn protruding from its forehead—somehow stems from this strange sea mammal.

Although narwhals have poor eyesight, they are difficult to hunt because of their extremely sharp hearing. At the slightest sound of a paddle, or of a foot-

A whale at bay is like a fighting mountain of fury.

step on the ice, they are off and away. The narwhal must be eaten as soon as it is killed, for the meat rapidly becomes poisonous.

How, one wonders, can there possibly be enough food in the polar seas to feed such an abundance of mighty creatures? Actually, life teems in northern waters, which are filled with countless organisms. Some of these are crustaceans—shellfish, crabs, snails. Others are tiny forms of plant life, known as diatoms. Many are so small that they can be seen only through a microscope. The common name for this form of sea life is plankton. It exists in unbelievable quantities. Almost without power of movement, plankton is carried automatically along in the ocean currents. Often it occurs in such masses that the water loses its customary blue color and becomes green or reddish-brown. The early whalemen quickly discovered that whales abounded where plankton was thickest. From this they deduced that the principal food of the whale and dolphin families must be plankton.

Fish have always been of utmost importance to the Eskimo—cod and halibut in the sea, salmon in rivers and lakes. For centuries the Greenlanders have pursued shark fishing. Although the Arctic shark reaches some

Creatures of the Arctic Sea

eighteen feet in length, it does not attack man. It swarms around the carcass of a dead whale or seal, greedily gorging itself until it can hardly swim. The chief value of the shark lies in its liver, from which a vitamin-rich oil is extracted.

The red char, a kind of salmon, is abundant in the Canadian Arctic, in Greenland, Spitsbergen and Novaya Zemlya.

The Arctic shark is sometimes eighteen feet in length.

8.

Arctic Birds That Come and Go

In the spring, many different species of birds migrate to the Arctic, some to within four hundred miles of the North Pole. A list of all or even a majority of these birds would fill many pages.

Arctic land birds are less numerous than those which snatch a living from the sea. The little snow bunting is the first bird to appear. In fact it is a late winter arrival rather than an early spring one. It is the only true songbird of the Arctic. With the exception of the bunting, seafowl put in an appearance long before the land species. Rocky ledges and cliffs rising from the sea are soon alive with countless thousands of nesting birds.

The coastal tundra is a haven for geese and ducks of all

Arctic Birds That Come and Go

sorts—black brant, pintails, mallards, and green-winged teal among others. Alaska's most beautiful goose, the emperor, nests along the Bering tidal lands and winters in the Aleutian Islands. The largest species of waterfowl in North America, the trumpeter swan, winters in southeastern Alaska. Its numbers today are diminishing rapidly.

Late spring finds huge flocks of blue geese flying in from James Bay and the mouth of the Mississippi, where they have wintered. The strange honking call of the lesser Canada goose competes with the trumpet-like cry of the sandhill crane. Red-throated loons wail their mournful cry from the thawing lake margins. Snowy owls hoot interminably; their hollow, booming note carries for a distance of six or seven miles. Long-tailed jaegers (a sort of hawklike gull) scream a cry as if they were saying *error error*—suggesting that everything in the world has gone wrong. The whistling swan flies high overhead, calling *woo-hoo woo-hoo*. Every bird that can hoot, scream or honk sets up its own peculiar cry. Horned larks pipe bravely above the bedlam created by their fellows. In spring, there is nothing silent about the so-called silent North!

Over the open pack ice, far from land, birds are

The long-tailed jaegers create havoc among smaller birds.

not often seen, for feeding is poor. The edge of the drift ice, however, is the favorite haunt of the fulmar, a sort of petrel as large as a gull. The auks fly wherever there is open water. So do the black guillemots and puffins, the ivory gulls and the kittiwakes. The long-tailed jaegers create havoc among the smaller birds. It is a common sight to see one of these hawklike gulls chase a Lapland longspur high into the sky, bite it in mid-air, pull out its tail feathers, follow it to the ground and devour it in a couple of gulps.

Of all waterfowl, the eider duck is most important to the hunter. Formerly vast quantities of eggs and

In early spring thousands of wild ducks fly north.

masses of eider down (the bird's soft breast feathers) were collected annually in Spitsbergen and Greenland. Eskimos placed great value on eider skins for clothing that is both light and warm. The number of these ducks has greatly decreased. It is estimated that fifty years ago 20,000 eiders were killed annually, and some 300,000 eggs were taken from Danish Greenland. The annual export of eider down for many years was over a ton and a half. Today the export is small, for the eider duck is protected by law.

Of all migratory birds, the Arctic tern is the most remarkable. It ranges from the Arctic all the way to

All About the Arctic and Antarctic

the Antarctic and back again. The tern appears to follow the light, leaving the Northland at the first hint of winter, crossing the vast Pacific Ocean to reach the Antarctic continent at the beginning of the southern summer. Seven months of this little bird's year are consumed in flight. With the sun shining through its thin wings, the tern travels thousands and thousands of miles every year.

When hunting, the Arctic tern is beautiful to watch. With red beak thrust downward, it sets its wings in preparation for a swift dive. Straight as an arrow it plunges into the water, to make off with a tiny stickleback that it swallows in mid-air. The little bird is handsome, too, with a pearly gray back and glossy black crown.

Almost as remarkable as the tern is the Pacific golden plover. This bird is a wader, not much larger than a robin. It passes the summer in the Aleutian Islands. At the first hint of approaching winter, small flocks of plover (many of them only three or four months old) go skimming along the ground in short trial flights. Suddenly some age-old instinct whips the flock up into the air. Higher and higher the plovers fly, to disappear over the wind-swept ocean to the south.

The golden plover flies 2,000 miles from the Arctic to Hawaii.

Forty hours later the flock makes its landfall in the Hawaiian Islands—a nonstop flight of more than 2,000 miles! Many of the birds fly on to New Zealand, resting along the way at some of the coral islands that dot the central Pacific. From the air these islands look like microscopic bits of coral. Locating them is considered something of an accomplishment for an airplane pilot with $10,000 worth of navigational equipment in the cockpit. How the little golden plover manages this remarkable feat, no one knows.

The mottled feathers of a ptarmigan are a perfect camouflage.

By the middle of June, all the land birds of the Arctic have made their nests and laid their eggs on the rolling, treeless tundra. Soon the eggs will be hatching, young birds will be trying their wings. The fledglings who survive their natural enemies—hawks, owls, foxes and weasels—will be gathering strength for the long southern migrations which begin in September.

The ptarmigan (a sort of partridge) does not migrate. It is one of the most important land birds of the North. With its mottled coat of brown, white and gray, this bird is perfectly camouflaged for its Arctic background. It looks for all the world like a bit of snowdrift nestled against brown grass and gray rock. Its tiny red comb is easily mistaken for a cluster of berries. Its legs and feet are feathered to the very claws. More

Arctic Birds That Come and Go

than any other Arctic creature, the ptarmigan wears the magic cloak of invisibility. Its chief enemy is the keen-eyed gerfalcon. Possibly because of its clever camouflage, the ptarmigan is the most self-confident of birds. It runs rather than flies from a man's approach. For this reason, Eskimos often are able to catch large numbers of these birds with an ordinary fish net.

The raven, the gerfalcon, the ptarmigan and the snowy owl are the only land birds which live in the Arctic all year. All others, of land or sea, take off at the first hint of northern sunset. And with their passing, a great silence settles once more over the lonely wastes of the Far North.

Like the snowy owl, the gerfalcon lives in the Arctic all winter.

9.

The Eskimo's Greatest Friend

In southeastern Alaska live the Tlingit Indian tribes, the Tsimshians, and a handful of Haidas. The Athabascans, who are trappers and caribou hunters, live in the interior. Today, little remains of the old Indian cultures. Eskimos and Indians belong to the same racial family. They are, you might say, first cousins. They have the same coppery skin, high cheekbones, straight black hair, and small slightly slanting black eyes. Unlike the Indian, however, the Eskimo still clings to many of his old ways.

The Eskimo's Greatest Friend

Most scientists believe that these people migrated to this continent from central Asia, possibly two thousand years ago. Crossing at Bering Strait, they spread out along the Alaska coast and the Canadian Arctic. Others pushed on across the frozen sea as far as Greenland. Still others moved south along the mainland of Canada to Labrador.

Although 6,000 miles of rugged land separate the Eskimo settlements of Alaska from those of Greenland, the language and customs still retain a remarkable similarity. There are about 40,000 Eskimos today, almost half of whom live in Alaska. Greenland, with some 16,000 is second in importance. All come under the rule of four different governments: the United States, Canada, Denmark and the Soviet Union.

The earliest Eskimo settlers quickly adapted themselves to cold and ice and snow. Their food was obtained almost solely by hunting, chiefly in the sea. Vegetable food, except for the mosses and berries of summer, was non-existent. Lacking metal of any sort, the Eskimos made weapons of bone or scraps of driftwood. For their frail craft they used skins stretched over frameworks of whalebone and sewn with sinews. For clothing, the furry hides of animals were ideal.

All About the Arctic and Antarctic

Shelters were constructed of stone, mud, hides or snow. Warmth and fuel could be found in the blubber of sea mammals, for seal or whale oil burns as well as kerosene.

Of necessity those early settlers were tough, clever and resourceful. Over the centuries they became accustomed to hardship. They learned to accept setbacks as a part of daily living. In the face of danger, pain or hunger, they were always ready with a joke or a laugh.

The Eskimo of today retains many of those qualities. He is invariably cheerful. He is also a born mechanic. Long before the coming of the white man he had invented a block and tackle with which to haul ashore the great weight of a walrus and drag it up on the ice for butchering. During World War II, engineers were frequently astonished at the skill with which an Eskimo could replace a piece of broken machinery with a part carved out of ivory.

By nature the Eskimo is a wanderer. He owns little but what he stands in and the tools with which he works. Trapping fields and hunting grounds are common property. Everyone may hunt where he likes; but it is the unwritten law of his race that every man and

The Eskimo's Greatest Friend

woman must work. There are few lazy men among them. The Eskimo, like the Indian, is an indulgent parent. He never punishes, seldom scolds a child. His theory is that the young will know hardship soon enough, and childhood is a time for play. Boys, following their fathers far out on the sea ice, learn to hunt at an early age. Girls, in imitation of their mothers, quickly acquire the skills needed for the rough life of the Eskimo woman.

In our cities people are exposed to all kinds of illnesses. This gives them a chance to build up resistance to disease. Before the coming of the white man, the Eskimo was superbly healthy. There were no germs in the cold air of the high North. Consequently the Eskimo had no immunity to the ailments introduced by the early whalers such as measles, tuberculosis and the common cold. Thousands of Eskimos have been killed by these illnesses.

Since there is relatively little vegetable food, the people of necessity are great meat eaters. They consume enormous quantities of seal and blubber. With a skinning-knife the Eskimo cuts off large chunks of meat and gulps it down—raw or half-cooked. This diet is supplemented by frozen fat and blood. Unpleasant as

All About the Arctic and Antarctic

it may sound, it is rich in vitamins. Nansen and Stefansson both have proved that even a white man can live in the Arctic and maintain health for long periods of time on meat alone.

The Eskimo calls his Husky dog *Kingmik*. The Husky is a mongrel made up of many different breeds. Some people believe he is related to the Arctic wolf. Like the wolf he never barks, he howls. But the ordinary Husky, with upstanding ears and a plumelike tail curving over his back, resembles rather such breeds as the Chow, the Newfoundland, the Labrador or the Spitz.

The dogs are born at any season of the year. A puppy comes into the world blind, but covered with hair. He opens his eyes on the seventh or eighth day. Bullied by the older dogs, pushed out into the cold world by his mother, he soon learns how to take care of himself. He is *always* hungry! He pounces upon anything edible, be it a sealskin mitt, a walrus-hide whip or a piece of harness. He wolfs it down as rapidly as possible before some larger dog can snatch it from him.

Huskies always sleep out of doors, even at 60° below zero. They lie buried in the snow which acts

The Husky never barks; he howls like a wolf.

as insulation against the cold. During the winter when the dog teams are working, they are fed every other day. In summer they are given virtually nothing to eat. Summer-born puppies find it difficult to keep alive. They roam the beaches, searching for any tidbit that might have been cast up by the waves. Feeding his dogs is one of the Eskimo's major problems, for a dog eats as much as a man. Often a party of hunters find themselves with a hundred hungry mouths to feed per day. The strain on both men and resources is enormous.

Sometimes the lead dog is at the head of a long towline.

Today an Eskimo needs many more dogs for hunting than his grandfather did. This is because modern firearms, ammunition and traps are much heavier equipment to transport than the old-time bows and arrows and spears.

Since the Eskimo is so dependent upon his dog team, he puts high value on a promising pup, even though he appears to neglect it. When about half-grown, the young Husky is broken to a harness made from strips of sealskin. Dog teams are not controlled by reins. They obey spoken commands and the crack of the long whip. In some parts of the Arctic, the lead dog is at the head of a long towline while the remaining dogs are paired

In the Hudson Bay area, the Huskies are hitched in fan shape.

behind him. This is called the Nome hitch. In the Hudson Bay region, as well as Greenland, the animals are hitched in fan shape. Generally there are from seven to fourteen dogs in a team. The leader is a privileged character, and he fights all others to hold his place. But if he misbehaves and is whipped by his master, he howls as if he were being killed by inches. The sled itself is usually ten or twelve feet long and three feet wide. It has high strong runners with handles at the back to help the driver steer.

The Husky is a born hunter. With his acute sense of smell, he can detect a herd of caribou many miles away. When hunting seals, the Eskimo allows his dogs

All About the Arctic and Antarctic

to wander where they will. Realizing that a capture means a meal for them, the Huskies are as eager as their masters in the successful outcome of the hunt. They race across the salt-water ice, sniffing at the cracks, while their master sends the lash of the walrus whip crackling above their ears.

The dogs are of great help to their owners in catching foxes. The trap line has to be visited at regular intervals, for wolves frequently eat the foxes as soon as they are caught. Again, ravens will steal the bait. When a snowstorm buries the traps many feet deep, the Husky's keen nose seeks them out. The Eskimo who puts out a line of a hundred or more traps needs all the help he can get from his faithful dogs.

Huskies always sleep out of doors, even at 60° below zero.

The Eskimo's Greatest Friend

The climax of a Husky's life is when he meets a polar bear face to face. The very scent of Nanook throws the whole dog team into a frenzy. Sometimes in the excitement of battle, a dog ventures too close to the bear's forepaws. He pays the penalty with his life. Death lies in Nanook's lightning-quick blows. By harrying at the bear's shaggy hindquarters the dogs hold the enemy at bay. But once they leap for Nanook's throat or ears, they are courting disaster.

No dog has greater endurance than the Husky. When the going gets roughest, when food is short or nonexistent, he will pull until he drops. Without this strange, mongrel breed of dog, the Eskimo **race** would long ago have vanished from the North.

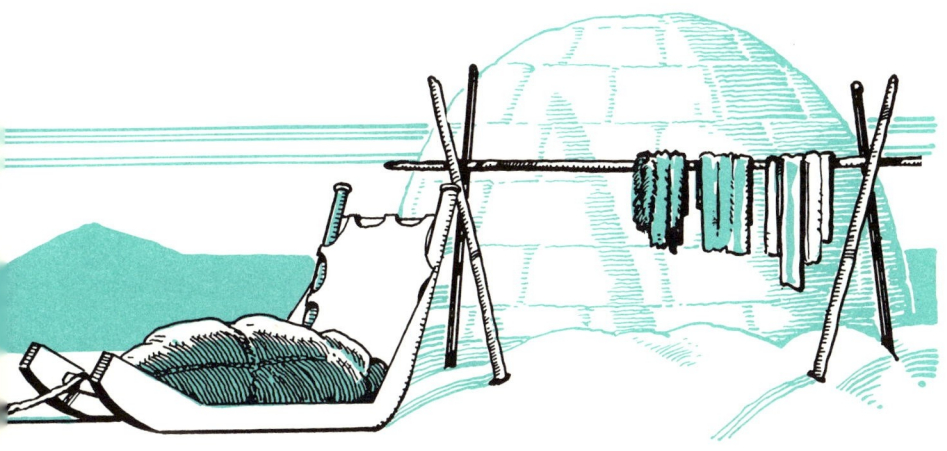

A hunter uses his igloo as a shelter when far from home.

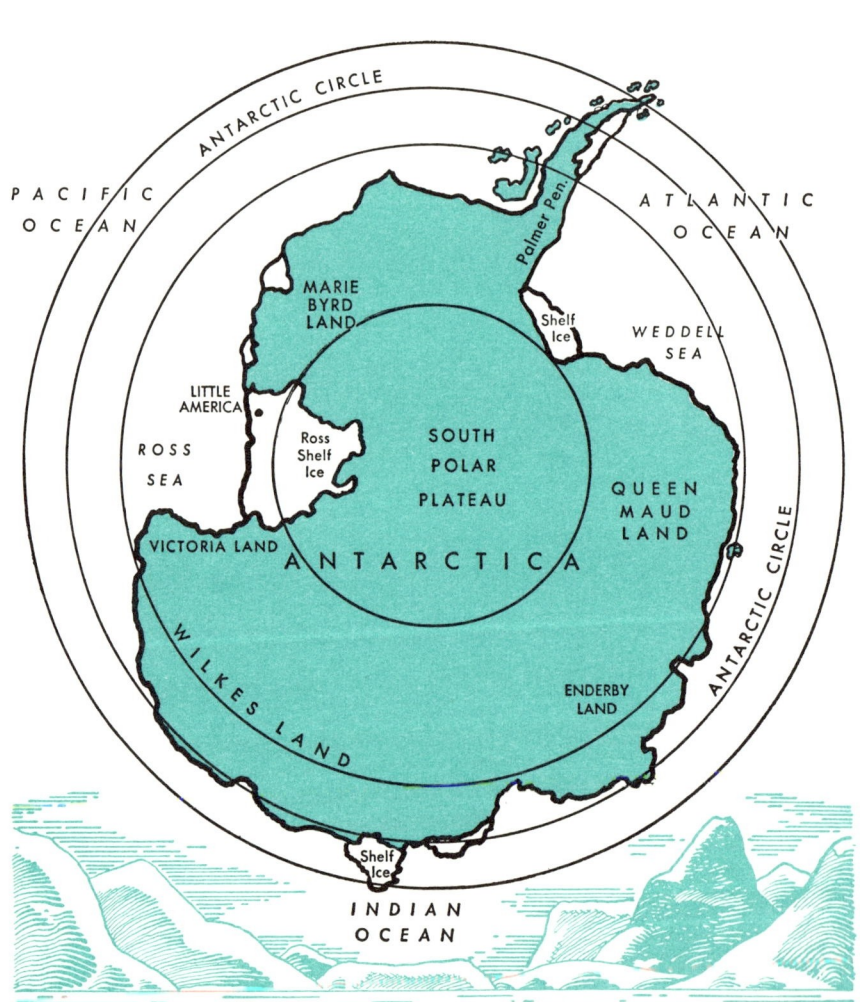

10.

Towering Peaks and Icy Depths

The difference between the Arctic and the Antarctic is the difference between life and death. For the South Pole is surrounded by an almost lifeless land mass. This southern continent is twice the size of the United States. It is roughly circular in shape with a narrow peninsula jutting northward toward South America. The average elevation of the interior is 7,500 feet above sea level. In the center is the South Pole, and from that point the only direction is north.

No region in the world is as cold as the Antarctic. Here temperatures often drop to 85° below zero. Winds up to 200 miles per hour howl through the per-

All About the Arctic and Antarctic

petual night of winter. Throughout the year temperatures remain near zero at the Pole. Even in midsummer the temperature of the Antarctic seldom rises above the freezing point of water. The average for the year is many degrees below that of the North Pole. This is because the Antarctic is a land mass surrounded by water while the North Polar Basin *is* water. And we know that water absorbs, retains, re-radiates whatever heat there may be.

No warm ocean currents ever reach the waters surrounding Antarctica. No tempering winds ever blow southward. Winters are unbelievably bitter.

The moisture of the continent is eternally frozen, hence rain is unknown. Even the snowfall is comparatively light. The only plants that find a foothold in the soil of this bleak region are tiny algae and sparse mosses and lichens. In the latter, a few tiny wingless insects struggle to exist during the summer.

Actually the white continent of the South Pole is geography's greatest unknown. Yet for centuries men have struggled to explore this area and to learn more about it.

We do know that it has not always been frozen waste. Scientists have discovered coal near the Beard-

Towering Peaks and Icy Depths

more Glacier. From this they know that in ancient times —perhaps 100,000,000 years ago—Antarctica was a land of forest and swamp. Dinosaurs and primitive mammals lumbered through its marshes. But no man's eye ever looked upon that surprising landscape, for it was long before the first human being appeared on earth. By the time man arrived in the world, Antarctica was covered with ice and snow.

Two hundred years ago scientists were convinced that this southern continent existed. They also believed it was inhabited by millions of human beings. But no one had ever been there to find out. In 1768 the British Admiralty sent Lieutenant James Cook on a voyage of discovery which, it was hoped, would settle the matter for all time. If the white continent really existed, it would be claimed in the name of the King of England.

Cook's orders read in part: "You are to observe the nature of the soil and the products thereof; the beasts and fowls that inhabit it. And in case you find any mines, minerals, or valuable stones, you are to bring home specimens of same. . . ."

Cook managed to sail farther south than any man before him—71° S. But after months of hardship, he was forced to abandon his search. The bitter cold and icy blasts convinced him that if there was a southern continent no human being could possibly live there.

Half a century later, twenty-one-year-old Nathaniel Palmer cruised the south polar waters in his own 47-foot sloop. Palmer, like the five men of his crew, came from Stonington, Connecticut. The young American captain was searching for seals. Instead, he found a part of the unknown continent—the long narrow peninsula now called Palmer Peninsula.

The young American charted the land he sighted and set sail for home. On the way he was overtaken by a warship flying the Russian Imperial flag and commanded by Admiral Bellingshausen. For two years the Admiral had been cruising along the edge of the ice pack, hoping to find land he could claim in the name of the Czar. After examining young Palmer's charts, the Russian officer realized that the American had been the first to discover this arm of land. Bellingshausen was forced to admit that he had arrived too late.

If you look at a modern map of Antarctica, you will see that a great area bears the name Wilkes Land. This is on the side facing Australia and washed by the Indian Ocean. It gets its name from Lieutenant Charles Wilkes, an American naval officer. In 1838 he left the United

Palmer cruised the south-polar waters in a 47-foot sloop.

States in command of five naval vessels. His orders were to chart the southernmost point of the globe.

Weeks dragged into months. Gales and mountainous seas beset the ships. Scurvy broke out on all five vessels. The dreaded south polar winter was at hand. Wilkes was a quarrelsome man, constantly at odds with his officers. His crew threatened mutiny. Harassed on all sides, the commander was forced to give the order to retreat. But before he turned homeward, Wilkes discovered the south polar continent proper. One area of this he christened "Adélie," in honor of his wife.

All About the Arctic and Antarctic

The following year a British expedition, under Sir James Clark Ross, sailed as far south as the present Ross Sea. This was the first time the towering mountain ranges of the western shore were discovered.

Then, for more than a century, the Antarctic remained a ghost land in which the outside world appeared to have lost interest.

Out of such sketchy beginnings, a picture of the Antarctic began to take shape. It would be difficult to imagine a more inhospitable continent. From the icy ramparts of the coast, the land slopes upward to the 10,000-foot plateau surrounding the South Pole. Back of the great cliffs lining the Ross Sea, mountains sweep skyward, range upon range. The Markhams, on the edge of Queen Maud Range, are over 15,000 feet high. Mount Kirkpatrick, in the same range, rises 14,624 feet —higher than our own Mount Whitney. Mount Lister, 13,350 feet, looms above the Ross Sea, with an active volcano called Erebus near by. Erebus itself is more than 13,000 feet high.

From the high plateau surrounding the South Pole, tremendous glaciers pour down through every valley. At the head of the Ross Sea stands the Beardmore Glacier, where the coal outcrops were first discovered. The glacier itself is 25 miles wide at the top, 8 miles wide at

Back of the Ross Sea, mountains sweep up, range on range.

All About the Arctic and Antarctic

the bottom, and roughly 100 miles long. Many other glaciers, equally impressive, pour down from the high plateau surrounding the South Pole.

Over the greater part of the Ross Sea, the icecap is a vast, slowly moving sheet of ice known as the Ross Ice Shelf. Approximately the size of France, this shelf is a floating extension of the Antarctic continent. It is fed by glaciers and creeps outward at the rate of 500 feet a year, covering the ocean for several hundred miles. The cap is possibly 1,500 feet thick, and its surface is relatively smooth. But where the icecap meets the continental slope, there is a barrier of ghastly crevasses. Some of these are visible. Others are wholly concealed by a coating of snow. The kick of a boot may open up a chasm hundreds of feet deep.

This barrier is the greatest hazard to the progress of modern explorers. The danger of moving heavy equipment over such an area was recently illustrated in a tragic manner. Members of the U. S. Army and Navy have been trying to find a route from the level Ross Ice Shelf (on which Admiral Byrd's "Little America" is built) up onto the Rockefeller Plateau of Marie Byrd Land. One of the ponderous D-8 tractors suddenly found the snow falling out from under its stern. The

Towering Peaks and Icy Depths

machine plunged backward into a deep crevasse, crushing the Navy Seabee who was trapped in the cab.

From the air you can see that these crevasses run in parallels, like waves moving toward the shore. Each wave has a crest, with a corresponding hollow between. Explorers seeking a path through this treacherous region are forced to walk the crest of the wave, so to speak.

Despite its perils, the Ross Ice Shelf is the best route to the South Pole because it is the shortest route. During the summer, ships can come through the Ross Sea to the Shelf. Then from the edge of the sea, it is only 800 miles across the Shelf and the mainland to the Pole.

11.

Exploring the World of the Antarctic

The South Pole itself has always been a symbol of courage and human endurance. The summer of 1911–12 saw two strikingly different men make a race to reach the Pole: Norway's Roald Amundsen and England's Sir Robert Falcon Scott.

Scott was a captain in the Royal Navy. A brief trip to the Antarctic in 1901 had fired him with the determination to reach the South Pole before any other explorer. Amundsen, who discovered the Northwest Passage in 1903, determined to be the first man to reach the North Pole. When he heard that Peary reached the Pole in 1909, he was bitterly disappointed. But the South Pole had not yet been attained, and Amundsen decided at once to make a dash for it. He was well aware that Scott also was outfitting for the same endeavor. It would be a close race for fame between two daring men.

From the beginning bad luck dogged the British expedition. Mistakenly Captain Scott tried to use Mongolian ponies to haul his sledges across the ice. They proved to be wholly unsuited to such a task. Some plunged through crevasses and were lost. Others froze or starved to death. On January 4th, Scott's supporting party—by this time thoroughly discouraged—returned to the base camp. But the leader himself, with only four companions, pushed doggedly ahead for the South Pole. No sign of Amundsen had been seen. Scott was confident that he would be the first to reach the Pole.

A bitter shock was in store for him. On the seventeenth day of January, a tent was discovered in the distance. Above it the flag of Norway streamed in the icy wind. Roald Amundsen and his men had reached their goal, staked their claim and departed! Inside the tent, Scott found some supplies and a note from the Norwegian explorer. This note was to be forwarded to the King of Norway in case Amundsen himself should perish on the return journey. The message was brief.

> Polheim, 15 December, 1911
> Dear Capt. Scott:
> As you are probably the first to reach this area after us, I will ask you kindly to forward this letter to King Haakon VII. If you can use any of the articles left in this tent, please do not hesitate to do so. The sledge left outside may be of use to you. With best regards I wish you safe return.
> Yours truly—Roald Amundsen

Bitterly disappointed, Scott and his four companions headed back toward the base camp. Eight months later, at the beginning of the Antarctic summer, their bodies were found. The Englishman's diaries filled in the details of the tragedy. It was a heroic story which has few equals in the history of exploration.

Amundsen's achievement should not be passed by briefly. Unlike Scott, the Norwegian had taken every precaution. On the way to the Pole he had erected snow beacons every three miles to serve as guideposts for the return journey. Provisions were cached every sixty miles. The Norwegians remained four days at the South Pole. Then, favored by fine weather, they found them-

Exploring the World of the Antarctic

selves back at their base camp within thirty-eight days. Every man was in splendid condition.

In such fashion the first great chapter of South Polar exploration came to a close.

In recent years the late Admiral Richard E. Byrd took the lead in probing the mysteries of Antarctica. His expeditions into this frozen world have added more to our knowledge of its geography than have those of any other man. He stands as one of the greatest explorers of all time.

Richard E. Byrd was born in Winchester, Virginia, in 1888. When he was only twelve years old, he made a trip around the world alone. This unusual adventure was prophetic of his whole future. Byrd graduated from the Naval Academy in 1912, trained as a World War pilot in 1917. Eight years later he served as flight commander with the Navy-Macmillan expedition to Greenland. In 1926, with Floyd Bennett as pilot, he accomplished the first flight to the North Pole. Never one to rest on his laurels, Byrd then flew his monoplane *America* across the Atlantic Ocean in 43 hours—a feat that barely escaped a tragic ending.

But it was in the frozen wastes of the Antarctic that Admiral Byrd found his greatest challenge. He led

All About the Arctic and Antarctic

four major expeditions into south polar regions, flying across the South Pole itself and penetrating the mysterious areas of the plateau. More than a quarter of the southern continent bears the name "Marie Byrd Land" in honor of his wife.

Admiral Byrd's third Antarctic expedition, 1939–41, was sponsored by the United States Government, and many important surveys were carried out at that time. A thousand miles of coastline and an additional 100,000 of surface were charted. Coal, copper, and other mineral deposits were reported.

But it was in Operation High Jump in 1947, Byrd's fourth expedition, that a scale was set which dwarfed all previous endeavors. Twelve Navy ships, 4,000 officers and men comprised the force. They were backed by the finest equipment developed for the Navy during World War II. This was the largest expedition to enter the Antarctic up to that time. It was on this expedition that Byrd made his second flight across the South Pole.

12.

Mysterious Sights and Sounds

Reports of South Pole explorers tell amazing tales of the strange phenomena that take place in the Antarctic. One of them appears when the wind-blown snow becomes charged with electricity. At such moments all pointed objects—a man's nose or his pipe, for example—glow with that same blue phantom light known to sailors as "St. Elmo's fire." The effect is weird and unearthly.

In this land of uniform whiteness, human eyesight frequently plays pranks; for the eye is scarcely better adjusted to complete whiteness than it is to total dark. Often men are bewildered by the abrupt disappearance of large moving objects which, only a second before, have been in full view. No satisfactory explanation for this occurrence has been found. It takes place only on what are known as "white" days—when air and ice and sky and whirling snow merge into a uniform blanket of whiteness. Surprisingly, at such times a severe case of sunburn becomes an Antarctic hazard. For there is no hiding from the invisible, ultraviolet radiation. It strikes from every angle, from every point of the compass.

On days of overcast, the uncertain light is trapped between the clouds above and the snow below. A thick, milky film forms in the atmosphere. This is known as a "white-out." Fliers caught in it may become dizzy and nauseated as they grope blindly for a surface on which to land. They may become hopelessly lost. All perspective vanishes. In a white-out it is impossible for a man to tell whether a dark spot forty feet ahead is a sled dog or a distant mountain.

The "loom" or mirage—so common in North Polar regions—is even more frequent and spectacular in the Antarctic. These mirages are sometimes blessings in disguise, for they enable the explorer to see objects lying far beyond the normal range of vision. The survivors of Scott's party in 1912, anxiously awaiting a rescue ship from New Zealand, first saw the masts towering un-

Mysterious Sights and Sounds

naturally high. Then the ship itself appeared in the sky —upside down! The men rejoiced, for they knew that help was just over the horizon.

Sometimes during the winter night the southernmost sky is festooned with flickering bands of pale, greenish light—the aurora australis. This electrical display is a counterpart of the northern lights of the Far North.

Almost directly above the South Pole, the two Clouds of Magellan may be seen. They are the most distant objects the human eye can reach—tremendous clusters of stars whose light (for almost a million years) has been traveling across outer space at a speed of 180,000 miles a second.

In the Antarctic, when the sun hangs low on the horizon, the sky frequently turns green—as green as a New England lawn in summer. This color reaches from the horizon halfway to the zenith—a violent sunset in shades of green. It is thought to be due to an electrical discharge from the vast numbers of ice particles in the atmosphere.

Halos around sun and moon are of common occurrence. And, surprisingly, in the Antarctic men breathe rainbows! The breath's moisture freezes instantly, forming clouds of ice crystals; sunlight turns them into mini-

All About the Arctic and Antarctic

ature rainbows that seem to emerge from a man's very lungs.

Strangely enough, everything that moves in the Antarctic seems to bear naturally to the left. A man and his dogs, lost in the snow, invariably circle in that direction. Snow whirls always to the left. Penguins, waddling to their rookeries, leave their tracks in the same direction. During the summer, for twenty-four hours a day the sun moves always from right to left.

In North Polar regions, as we have seen, the reverse takes place. Instinctively man, bird and beast seem to turn right north of the equator, and left south of the equator.

In the Antarctic, temperatures have been recorded of 120° below zero. But there, when a man breathes this air, he can *hear* his breath as well as see it. As the frozen moisture drifts from mouth and nose, its ice crystals break against his ears with a tinkling sound of tiny bells. Such temperatures are the dread of the modern explorer, who watches his precious kerosene pour like oil, oil like molasses. When lubricants congeal, machines wear out quickly. Engine metal becomes brittle. Electrical systems go awry when their rubber protection disintegrates in the bitter cold.

Mysterious Sights and Sounds

From the last week in March to the last week in September, the Antarctic is wrapped in twilight or darkness. At the Pole, from the end of September to the end of March the sun never sets. Both perpetual light and perpetual dark play havoc with the sleep mechanism of human beings, sometimes harrying them almost beyond endurance.

The Antarctic is germ free. There are no bacteria to spoil food, no spores in the air to molder bread. All food freezes solid and remains for many years in a state of remarkable preservation. One of Admiral Byrd's trail parties ate and enjoyed 30-year-old supplies that had been left behind by Amundsen. In 1947 Rear Admiral Curzon landed by helicopter near the camp site abandoned by Robert Scott thirty-five years earlier. Instead of being storm-ridden and dilapidated, as would have been the case in a temperate climate, the camp appeared as fresh as if its occupants had left only the day before. Timber that had gone into the cabin's construction looked as though it had just come from the sawmill. There was not a rusty nail, no sign of rot in the beams. Canned beef and biscuits had retained their flavor. The leather harness of the Mongolian ponies was still as tough as hemp. A sled dog that had frozen to death while standing looked as if it was about to spring into action.

The wind that blows forever northward from the South Pole is the earth's driest, purest air. Sterilized by vast quantities of ultraviolet, it is radiated throughout the three months of summer. No child has yet been born in the Antarctic; but one such might pass his whole life in a sterilized world. No measles, mumps or chicken pox; no scarlet fever, colds or "flu." Having built up no resistance to disease, however, such a child would certainly succumb to any illness introduced from the outside world.

13.

Antarctic Wild Life

The only mammals of the Antarctic live in the sea. There are five kinds of seals. These are of the "hair" variety, whose hides are of no value. Their flesh is fit only for dog food.

The Weddell seal is commonest. Found on or near all Antarctic shores, it reaches nine feet in length and 900 pounds in weight. It lives in colonies, buried under the ice all winter; and like all other mammals and birds of the south polar regions, it shows no fear of man.

The white crab-eater seal is slimmer and more active than the Weddell seal. It never travels in herds, living a solitary life on the ice floes of the open ocean. Like

All About the Arctic and Antarctic

the Ross seal (the rarest of all) almost nothing is known about its habits.

The green-bellied seal is another rare mammal. When attacked, its head can be almost completely withdrawn inside a thick, bloated neck. This seal inhabits the pack ice and rarely is found more than a few feet from the water. It emits a high, chirping call, similar to that of a bird.

One of the most dangerous mammals that exists is the sea leopard. Due to its great size and weight, it is even more dangerous than the animal for which it is named. It is of the seal family and grows to a length of ten feet, with a five-foot girth. Though it lives chiefly on penguins, it is capable of killing other seals larger than itself. It can travel over rough ice faster than a man can run. The earliest Antarctic explorers brought home tales of the savagery of this beast, but no sea leopard has ever been taken alive.

The grampus, or killer whale, which also exists in the Arctic, frequents the Ross and Weddell seas. He is just as ferocious in the Antarctic as in the north polar region.

The true whales of the Antarctic belong to two major groups. First in importance are the fin whale and

When a whale surfaces, it is like a giant torpedo shooting up.

the blue whale, generally called the sulphur-bottom. These are baleen whales because their mouths are equipped with hairy, bristly plates known as baleen. These creatures live on tiny shrimplike crustaceans, called krill, that float in the water. The whale opens its great mouth and takes in a vast quantity of water containing thousands of krill. Then it closes its jaws, and the water squeezes through the baleen plates. Thus the tiny shrimp are left for the great whale to swallow whole.

The sulphur-bottom is the largest animal that ever lived, even larger than the dinosaurs that roamed the earth millions of years ago. The longest one ever measured was 111 feet, with its head taking up almost half of its length. Dark gray-blue in color it has white spots on its belly. Usually its weight is estimated at a ton per foot of length.

The sulphur-bottom's closest rival in size is the fin whale. It seldom exceeds 90 feet in length and is more slender in build. Usually it does not go as far south as the ice pack.

The second important group of whales is known as the toothed whales. These have no baleen plates. They do have small peglike teeth. The largest and most important of this group is the sperm whale, measuring up to sixty feet in length. A square-headed, square-jawed monster, it is usually coal-black in color. When pursued and harpooned, the sperm whale puts up a heroic battle for life. Its average rate of speed is from 10 to 12 knots,

Emperor penguins stand more than four feet high.

but when frightened it may possibly achieve as much as 20 knots—an astonishing speed for a monster of such size.

The outstanding citizens of manless Antarctica are birds that look absurdly like men: penguins. Of the several varieties, the emperor penguin is the most un-

All About the Arctic and Antarctic

usual. Standing four feet or more in height, weighing up to eighty pounds, these creatures appear to wear black coats, yellowish waistcoats, and orange-stained beaks. They walk with pompous gravity, bow to one another, and appear to be making solemn speeches. Now and again they give vent to a trumpet-like command.

Millions of years ago, as the Ice Age descended upon the Antarctic, animals and birds either migrated or became extinct. The penguin could not fly and was unable to swim great distances. Thus it was trapped eternally in an icy graveyard; but being of cold-blooded, reptilian ancestry, it was able to adjust to the slowly changing climate.

The emperor hen lays and hatches her single egg on the bare ice. There is no shelter from the wind and the temperature may be 80° below zero. The mother holds the newly-hatched chick in a fold of heavily feathered skin—somewhat like a kangaroo's pouch. Both parents take part in caring for the young, replacing one another for brief periods of food and rest.

Once past the chick stage, the infant emperor becomes one of the toughest creatures alive. Attacked by a sea leopard (its chief enemy), it often endures terrible wounds without succumbing. Seemingly awkward, the

The arctic tern ranges from Arctic to Antarctic and back.

penguin's flippers are capable of inflicting a quick and powerful blow—strong enough to break a man's arm.

Although the penguin is the best-known bird of the Antarctic, there are many others which more closely resemble our idea of what a bird should be. By far the most common of these is the snow petrel. Its snow-white plumage is almost invisible against its natural background of ice and snow. Its black eyes, black bill and feet stand out in sharp contrast. The snow petrel nests in the Antarctic regions; but as winter comes on,

The albatross may have a wingspread of ten or twelve feet.

Antarctic Wild Life

it flies into the Northern Hemisphere. Most of this long journey is over water, where the petrel seems completely at home. During the day it darts quickly and lightly over the waves. At night it nestles down on the water to rest.

Another great traveler among the sea birds is the arctic tern. This graceful little bird flies farther in its migration than any other bird known. Each year it travels from the North Pole to the South Pole, a distance of some 22,000 miles. It seems to follow the light, fleeing the northern Arctic winter to enjoy the brief Antarctic summer. In late February, at the first indication of the south polar sunset, the arctic tern heads north again.

Another famous traveler is the wandering albatross. It circles the globe in far southern latitudes. Superstitious sailors have long believed that the albatross brings good luck to a ship but misfortune to any man who kills one. Among the largest of all flying birds, the albatross has a wingspread of ten to twelve feet. It is clumsy on land, but in the air it is a miracle of grace. The albatross flies with the greatest of ease at 60 miles an hour. With a favorable wind, that speed may reach as much as 100 miles an hour.

All About the Arctic and Antarctic

The fiercest of Antarctic birds is the south polar skua. It is a hawklike gull, brownish-black and slightly larger than a pigeon. The moment a man steps on Antarctic ice he is surrounded by these fierce, bloodthirsty birds. Born robbers, they swoop down on colonies of penguins, killing as they go. A wounded seal is instantly hacked to pieces by the skuas' sharp beaks and claws. This vicious bird shows no fear of man.

The boldest of birds is the wide-winged giant fulmar. Heavily built, it has a wingspread that reaches seven feet. It will attack a man without hesitation, clawing at his eyes.

Antarctica is also the home of the stormy petrels, sometimes called "Mother Carey's chickens." Dark-brown and square-tailed, they are predominantly sea birds, but sometimes they are seen 100 miles inland. Sometimes flocks of these little birds will follow a ship for miles.

One of the strangest of all south polar winged creatures is the whalebird. This curious bird belongs to the petrel family. It is distinguished by a sieve of whalebone, or baleen, suspended from the upper jaw. This sieve strains particles of plankton from the sea after the fashion of the great whale.

Antarctic Wild Life

You might assume that in the bitter cold of the Antarctic no plants could survive. As a matter of fact, there seems to be an inexhaustible supply of sea plants. Most of them are so tiny that the finest microscope is needed to study them. No one can explain how these microscopic plants of the Antarctic seas survive six months of darkness during the south polar winter. But survive they do and thus provide food for some of the world's largest mammals. For in Antarctic waters vast herds of whales and porpoises gorge themselves on these tiny floating plants. And when we realize that one of these creatures may require more than a ton of food each day, we get some idea of the quantity of plants available.

Fish of many kinds abound in the same waters in which the microscopic plants flourish. There are starfish, jellyfish and squids. There are small octopi that float on the surface. And there are acres of tiny pink shrimp or krill that drift with the current until some great sulphur-bottom whale gulps up the next mouthful of his midday lunch.

14.

Operation Deep-Freeze

Of late, Antarctica has bustled with unaccustomed life and color. For many nations of the world have cooperated in a gigantic project to learn more about this area and about the earth in general. The period from July, 1957, to December, 1958—called the International Geophysical Year—was named as the time for this great scientific undertaking. Eleven nations besides the United States set up thirty-nine bases on Antarctica. At these bases scientists kept careful records of every aspect of the weather, the climate and the heavens, of gravity and electricity, of earthquakes and magnetism, of the ocean

Operation Deep-Freeze

and the rocky crust of the earth. Parties went out from the bases to gather more data. Operation Deep-Freeze was one of the largest scientific undertakings in history.

The nations taking part in the enterprise were Britain, France, the Soviet Union, Norway, Australia, New Zealand, Argentina, Chile, South Africa, Belgium, Japan and the United States.

America's contribution to the project began with seven ships, carrying 1,800 men, and led by the icebreaker, *U.S.S. Glacier*. The expedition—Task Force 43—was under command of Rear Admiral George Dufek, with Admiral Byrd as overall director. Its mission was to set up two bases on the edge of the continent, at Ross Island and Little America—800 miles from the pole. There 165 volunteers would spend the winter after establishing a beachhead.

In December, 1955, the *Glacier*—an 8,000-ton monster of 21,000 horsepower—slashed its way through ice 15 feet thick. It hammered into the Ross Sea ice pack at 17 knots. When it failed to shatter the ice in frontal attack, it rode upon the floes and crushed them with its ponderous weight. In this manner a 400-mile passage was cleared to the lofty ice cliffs that border the Ross Sea shoreline.

Outposts were established in the Antarctic for scientists.

Construction crews swarmed ashore at McMurdo Sound and Little America. The rat-tat of hammers, the whine of saws, the growling of jeeps and tractors shattered the Antarctic stillness. Little communities of multicolored polar huts sprang up from the snow. They would be the home for many months to come of American scientists and Seabees.

The building of the bases was a race against time and against the elements, for the scientists had to be at their instruments when International Geophysical Year

Operation Deep-Freeze

began. The McMurdo base had to be ready to handle air traffic by the time the Antarctic summer returned in October. In two 12-hour shifts a day the men labored under floodlights, in temperatures as low as 69° below zero. Tractors dragged load after load of supplies from the water's edge, across miles of ice veined with treacherous cracks.

On October 16, 1956, the job was completed. Operation Deep-Freeze swung into high gear. Task Force 43 poured supplies and men ashore at the two Ross Sea bases. From Little America a tractor train drove deep into the unknown fastnesses of Marie Byrd Land, to set up a year-round base. Long-range planes, flown in from New Zealand, made many trips into the interior, scouting nearly one-third of the continent's hitherto unmapped territory.

Not long after this, Rear Admiral Dufek became the first man in forty-six years to stand on the ice of the South Pole. With the temperature at 58° below zero, he was landed by a twin-engined ski-equipped Navy R4D transport plane named *Que Será, Será*. His plane was escorted to the Pole by a giant Air Force C-124 Globemaster. The escort plane did not land, but circled constantly, giving navigational help.

The Stars and Stripes were run up at the South Pole.

Operation Deep-Freeze

The polar plateau at this point is 10,300 feet above sea level. Immediately upon landing, Admiral Dufek chopped a hole in the ice with an Alpine ice ax and raised the Stars and Stripes. Into the bamboo flagstaff he placed a note, testifying to his presence. Then he directed the laying out of radar reflectors and other equipment which would make the spot easier to find in the future.

This accomplished, he climbed back into the plane whose motors were still purring. But when the pilot gunned his engines and fired four JATO (jet assist) bottles for take-off, the *Que Será, Será* refused to budge. Its skis were frozen solid to the South Pole's icy surface. It took all of the eleven remaining JATO bottles to blast the plane loose. At well below normal take-off speed, it lurched and staggered up into the thin air of 10,000 feet.

Of all the nations taking part in the conquest of Antarctica, the United States has the largest investment in men, money and machines. Admiral Dufek's pioneer landing laid the groundwork for the cluster of orange and tan huts now standing at 90° S.—the point at which all meridians converge, from which all directions are north: the mathematical bottom of the earth.

All About the Arctic and Antarctic

It is here that Paul Siple, geographer and explorer, landed for a 14-month stay at the most isolated community on earth. Siple first visited Antarctica as a Sea Scout with Admiral Byrd's 1928–30 expedition. He was a member of four later parties. This south polar veteran directed the research activities of a group of American scientists—four meteorologists, a glaciologist, a seismologist, and several upper-atmosphere specialists. They dug deep into the Antarctic's frozen crust, probed high into its icy upper atmosphere in their effort to answer secrets hidden for millions of years in the ancient ice and stormy skies of the white continent.

Many years will pass before we know what the scientists of the world learned during Operation Deep-Freeze at the South Pole. Even when their reports are made, we can be almost sure that the land of towering peaks and snowy depths will remain untamed and unsubdued.

Index

Aklavik, Canada, 68, 70
Alaska, 3, 5, 75
  birds of, 85
  crops in, 8
  and DEW Line, 12
  Eskimos in, number of, 93
  mammoth fossils in, 56
  heat in, 13-14
  natural resources of, 44*ff.*
  purchase price of, 44
  reindeer of, 69
  whale along coast of, 78
Alaska Highway, 50
Albatross, 130, 131
Aleutian Islands, 75, 85, 88
America (monoplane), 115
Amundsen, Roald, 112, 113, 114, 121
Antarctica, Adélie area of, 107
  in ancient times, 105
  bases on, 134, 136, 137
  early exploration of, 105-08
  germs absent in, 121*f.*
  mysteries of, 115, 117*ff.*
  and nations participating in Operation Deep Freeze, 135, 139
  Operation Deep Freeze in, 134-40
  and Ross Ice Shelf, 110*ff.*
  summer in, 122, 131
  sunsets absent in, 121
  temperatures in, 120, 128, 137
  wild life of, 123-33
  and Wilkes Land, 106
  winter in, 104
Arctic Archipelago, 49

Arctic Circle, 3, 4, 13, 35, 44, 45
Arctic Circle Exploration Company, 46
"Arctic Ocean," renaming of, 5
Arctic (Polar) Sea, 5, 6, 28, 66
  animal life in, 71-83
Asbestos, tremolite, 46
Aurora australis, 119
Aurora borealis, 8, 36
Autumn, Arctic, 32*ff.*
Aviation, Arctic, 10-11

Baffin Island, 35*ff.*, 41*ff.*
Bahr, Andrew, 68, 69
Baleen, 77, 78, 125
Bearded seal, 72, 74
Beardmore Glacier, 104-05, 108
Bellingshausen, Admiral, 106
Beluga, 78-79
Bennett, Floyd, 115
Birds, Arctic, 25, 34, 84-91
Bismuth, 45, 51
Blue whale, 125
Bowhead whale, 78
Bristol Bay, 46
Brooks Range, 45
Bunting, snow, 84
Byrd, Richard E., 110, 115, 116, 121, 135, 140

Canada, 3, 8, 32, 35
  Eskimos of, 93
  hare of, 65
  natural resources of, 49*ff.*
  newest railway in, 52
  Northwest Territories of, 49

Index

red char of, 83
reindeer of, 69
Cape Farewell, 55
Caribou, 65-68
Cartier, Jacques, 52
Char, red, 83
Chimo, Labrador, 53
Chinook salmon, 46
Clouds of Magellan, 119
Coal deposits, 45, 49, 54, 116
Cobalt, 51
Compass, 10, 11
Cook, James, 105
Copper, 44, 45, 53, 116
Cornwallis Island, 21
Crab-eater seal, 123
Crops, Arctic, 8, 28-29
Crustaceans, 82, 125
Cryolite, 55
Curzon, Rear Admiral, 121

DEW Line, 12
Diatoms, 82
Dog, of Eskimo, 96-101
Dolphin, 79, 82
Dufek, George, 135, 137, 139

Echo Bay, 51
Eggs, in Eskimo diet, 26
Eider duck, 86-87
Emperor penguin, 127-29
Erebus volcano, 108
Eskimos, appearance of, 92
  diet of, 26, 33, 67, 72, 95
  diseases acquired from white man, 95
  early, 93-94
  eider skins valued by, 87
  fish of importance to, 82

hare skin for boots of, 65
and Husky, 96-101
igloos built by, 38-41
Indians racially related to, 92
ivory carvings by, 56
kayaks of, 67
meat consumed by, 26, 33, 95
as mechanics, 94
migration from central Asia, 93
number of, in Alaska and Greenland, 93
as parents, 95
parkas of, 8, 15, 17
polar bear hunted by, 59
ptarmigan caught by, 91
reindeer cared for, 69
seal hunted by, 29, 32, 37, 38, 99-100
tents of, 23
umiaks of, 32, 36, 77
as wanderers, 94
weapons of, 98
whale killed by, 79

"Featherbone," 78
Fin whale, 124, 126
Fish, Antarctic, 133
Fishing industry, in Alaska, 46
Flowers, Arctic, 26, 27
Fort Yukon, 13
Fox, Arctic, 38, 59-61, 100
Franklin district, Northwest Territories, 49
Fulmar, giant, 132
Fur seal, 75

Gerfalcon, 34, 91
Glacier, 18
Glacier, U.S.S., 135

Index

Gold mines, 44, 49
Goose, Arctic, 34, 84, 85
Grand Falls, Labrador, 54
Great Bear Lake, 50, 51
Green-bellied seal, 124
Green sky, in Antarctic, 119
Greenland, 3, 5, 8, 10, 13, 54
  bowhead whale of, 78
  cryolite mined in, 55
  and DEW Line, 12
  and dogs in fan-shaped hitch, 99
  eider duck of, 87
  Eskimos in, number of, 93
  hare of, 65
  icecap in, 18
  musk ox of, 62
  Navy-Macmillan expedition to, 115
  polar bear of, 57
  red char of, 83
  and seal hunting, 74
  whale of, 77
Greenland Sea, 6
Gulf Stream, 5, 54
Gyro, Polar Path, 11

Hair seal, 74, 123
Hare, white Arctic, 64, 65
Hudson Bay, 78, 99
Hudson's Bay Company, 60
Hunting, by Eskimos, 29, 32, 37, 38, 59, 93, 98, 99-100
Husky, 96-101

Iceberg, 16, 18, 19
Icecap, Antarctic, 18
  Greenland, 118
Ice Pack, Polar, 4, 5
Igloo, 38-41

Indians, Arctic, 25, 92
Insects, Antarctic, 104
  Arctic, 31-32
International Geophysical Year, 134, 136
Iron deposits, 49, 52, 53

Jade deposits, 46
Jaeger, long-tailed, 86

Kayak, 67
Keewatin district, Northwest Territories, 49
Killer whale, 79-80, 124
King Charles Island, 57
Kingmik (husky), 96-101
Kirkpatrick, Mount, 108
Knob Lake, Labrador, 52
Krill, 125, 126, 133

LaBine, Gilbert, 50, 51
Labrador, 51-54, 74, 93
Lapland, 69
Lead deposits, 45, 49
Leftward motion, in Antarctic, 120
Lemming, 25, 34, 65
Lister, Mount, 108
Little America, 110, 135, 136, 137
Loom, 16, 118

Mackenzie district, Northwest Territories, 49
McMurdo base, 136, 137
Magellan, Clouds of, 119
Mammoth fossils, 55-56
Marie Byrd Land, 110, 116, 137
Markham Mountains, 108
Miass, cryolite mined at, 55

Index

Midnight sun, 7
Migratory birds, 25, 34, 85, 87ff.
Mineral deposits, in Alaska, 45
   in Canada, 49
Mirage, 15, 118
Mongolian ponies, 113, 121
Mosquitoes, Arctic, 31, 32
Musk ox, 61-62
Muskrat, 70

Nanook, 57-59, 101
Nansen, 9, 16, 96
Narwhal, 80, 82
Newfoundland, 74
Nome hitch, 99
Norman Wells, Canada, 49
North Pole, 3, 104, 113, 131
   air route over, 9-12
   first flight to, 115
   hair seal of, 74
   and Peary Land, 55
   in relation to sun, 6-7
   temperatures at, 13
Northwest Passage, 113
Northwest Territories, of Canada, 49
Norway, 54, 55, 113, 135
Novaya Zemlya, 83

Octopi, Antarctic, 133
Oil, in Alaska, 45
   in Canada, 49-50
Oimekon, Siberia, 13, 14
Okhotsk Sea, 78
Operation Deep Freeze, 134-40
Operation High Jump, 116
Ovibos, 61
Owl, snowy, 34, 91

Palmer, Nathaniel, 106
Parka, 8, 15, 17
Peary, North Pole reached by, 113
Peary Land, Greenland, 55
Penguin, 120, 124, 127-29, 132
Permafrost, 21
Petrel, snow, 129-30
   stormy, 132, 133
Pike's Peak, cryolite mined at 55
Pitchblende, 51
Plankton, 82, 132
Plants, Antarctic, 104, 133
   Arctic, 9, 26-27
Platinum, 45
Plover, Pacific golden, 88-89
Point Barrow, 45
Polar Basin, 4, 5, 6, 8, 47, 104
   polar bear of, 57
   seal of, 72
   thickness of ice in, 20
Polar bear, 57-59, 101
Polar Ice Pack, 4, 5
Polar Path Gyro, 11
Polar Sea, *see* Arctic Sea
Porpoise, 79, 133
Port Radium, 50
Pribilof, Gerasmin, 75
Ptarmigan, 34, 90-91
Pulpwood, of Labrador, 54

Que Será, Será, 137, 139
Queen Maud Range, 108

Radioactive minerals, 50, 51
Radium, 51
Raven, 34, 91, 100
Red char, 83

144

Index

Reindeer, 68-69
Resolute Bay, 21
Ringed seal, 72
Rockefeller Plateau of Marie Byrd Land, 110
Ross, James Clark, 108
Ross Ice Shelf, 110, 111
Ross Island, 135
Ross Sea, 108, 109, 110, 124, 135, 137
Ross seal, 124

St. Elmo's fire, 117
St. Lawrence Seaway, 53
Salmon catch, in Alaska, 46
Scott, Robert Falcon, 112, 113, 114, 118, 121
Sea leopard, 124, 128
Seal(s), 29, 30, 32, 33, 36, 37, 38, 71-76, 123-24
Settlement, Arctic, 47-48
Shark, Arctic, 82-83
Shungnak area, of Arctic, 46
Siberia, 3, 5, 13, 14, 47, 55
Silver deposits, 45, 51
Siple, Paul, 140
Skua, 132
Slush ice, 20
Snow bunting, 84
Snow petrel, 129-30
South Pole, 103, 108, 110, 111, 112, 113, 117, 131
  Byrd's flights across, 116
  Dufek at, 137
  Operation Deep Freeze at, 140
  pureness of air at, 122
  reached by Amundsen, 114
  Stars and Stripes raised at, 138, 139

temperatures at, 104, 137
Sperm whale, 126
Spitsbergen, 54, 57, 61, 83, 87
Spring, Arctic, 23ff.
Stefansson, 9, 29, 32, 96
Stickleback, 24
Stock farming, Arctic, 29
Stormy petrel, 132, 133
Sulphur-bottom whale, 125, 126 133
Summer, Antarctic, 122, 131
  Arctic, 24ff.
Sunburn, as Antarctic hazard, 118

Temperatures, Antarctic, 103, 104, 120, 128, 137
  Arctic, 13-15, 16, 28, 69, 96
Tern, Arctic, 87-88, 131
Thompson, David, 68
Toothed whale, 126
Trapping, in Arctic, 38, 70, 100
Trees, of Alaska, 46-47
Tremolite asbestos, 46
Tundra, 4

Umiak, 32, 36, 77
Ungava Bay, 53
Uranium, 49, 51

Verkhoyansk, Siberia, 14

Walrus, 76-77
Weather, Antarctic, 134ff.
  Arctic, 13ff.
Weddell seal, 123
Whale, 77-79, 124-27, 133
Whalebird, 132
Whalebone, 77, 78
White Alice, 12

Index

White crab-eater seal, 123
White-out, 118
White whale, 78-79
Whitehorse, Canada, 49
Wilkes, Charles, 106, 107
Wilkes Land, 106

Winter, Antarctic, 104
    Arctic, 35*ff*.
Wolf, Arctic, 62-64, 96

Yellowknife, Canada, 49
Yukon River, 78-79

Allabout Books

ANIMALS AND PLANTS

All About Animals and Their Young *by Robert M. McClung*
All About Horses *by Marguerite Henry*
All About Dogs *by Carl Burger*
All About Monkeys *by Robert S. Lemmon*
All About Elephants *by Carl Burger*
All About Whales *by Roy Chapman Andrews*
All About Fish *by Carl Burger*
All About Birds *by Robert S. Lemmon*
All About the Insect World *by Ferdinand C. Lane*
All About Moths and Butterflies *by Robert S. Lemmon*
All About Snakes *by Bessie M. Hecht*
All About Dinosaurs *by Roy Chapman Andrews*
All About Strange Beasts of the Past *by Roy Chapman Andrews*
All About Strange Beasts of the Present *by Robert S. Lemmon*
All About the Flowering World *by Ferdinand C. Lane*

EARTH SCIENCE

All About the Planet Earth *by Patricia Lauber*
All About Mountains and Mountaineering *by Anne Terry White*
All About Volcanoes and Earthquakes *by Frederick H. Pough*
All About Rocks and Minerals *by Anne Terry White*
All About the Ice Age *by Patricia Lauber*
All About the Weather *by Ivan Ray Tannehill*
All About Maps and Mapmaking *by Susan Marsh*
All About the Sea *by Ferdinand C. Lane*
All About Sailing the Seven Seas *by Ruth Brindze*
All About Undersea Exploration *by Ruth Brindze*
All About Great Rivers of the World *by Anne Terry White*
All About the Jungle *by Armstrong Sperry*
All About the Desert *by Sam and Beryl Epstein*
All About the Arctic and Antarctic *by Armstrong Sperry*

SPACE SCIENCE
All About Satellites and Space Ships *by David Dietz*
All About Rockets and Space Flight *by Harold L. Goodwin*
All About Aviation *by Robert D. Loomis*
All About the Planets *by Patricia Lauber*
All About the Stars *by Anne Terry White*
All About the Universe *by David Dietz*

PHYSICAL SCIENCE
All About the Atom *by Ira M. Freeman*
All About Electricity *by Ira M. Freeman*
All About Radio and Television *by Jack Gould*
All About Fire *by Raymond Holden*
All About Engines and Power *by Sam and Beryl Epstein*
All About the Wonders of Chemistry *by Ira M. Freeman*
All About Sound and Ultrasonics *by Ira M. Freeman*

BIOLOGY AND PSYCHOLOGY
All About Biology *by Bernard Glemser*
All About Heredity *by Judith Randal*
All About the Human Body *by Bernard Glemser*
All About the Human Mind *by Robert M. Goldenson*

GREAT DISCOVERIES
All About Great Medical Discoveries *by David Dietz*
All About Famous Scientific Expeditions *by Raymond P. Holden*
All About Famous Inventors and Their Inventions *by Fletcher Pratt*

MAN'S PAST
All About Prehistoric Cave Men *by Sam and Beryl Epstein*
All About Archaeology *by Anne Terry White*

THE UNITED STATES
All About Our 50 States *by Margaret Ronan*
All About the U. S. Navy *by Edmund L. Castillo*
All About Courts and the Law *by Ruth Brindze*

MUSIC
All About the Symphony Orchestra *by Dorothy Berliner Commins*